Embracing the Call to Spiritual Depth

Gifts for Contemplative Living

TILDEN EDWARDS

Paulist Press
New York/Mahwah, NJ

3|12

Cover design by Sharyn Banks
Book design by Lynn Else

Library of Congress Cataloging-in-Publication Data

Edwards, Tilden.
    Embracing the call to spiritual depth : gifts for contemplative living / Tilden Edwards.
        p. cm.
    Includes bibliographical references (p.   ).
    ISBN 978-0-8091-4627-7 (alk. paper)
    1. Christian life—Anglican authors. 2. Contemplation. I. Title.
    BV4509.5.E393 2010
    248.3′4—dc22
                                                                2009050895

Published by Paulist Press
997 Macarthur Boulevard
Mahwah, New Jersey 07430

www.paulistpress.com

Printed and bound in the
United States of America

Contents

iii

CONTENTS

Dedication

To my wife, Mary, who has shown me what love can be,
a love grounded in the larger Love that would
shine through all that is.
May that awesome Love draw all of us further into
its life-transforming radiance.

Acknowledgments

I am deeply indebted to my beloved and perceptive wife, Mary, for her steady support of this book, both personally and editorially. Her many suggestions along the way were invaluable. I am also grateful to David Keller for his valuable suggestions and encouragement related to the chapters on seminaries and congregations, and to Ann Dean for her insightful review of the section on contemplative awareness and the Earth. Monika Megyesi has given generously of her time and talent in formatting the manuscript. Then there is my learning from over thirty-five years of stimulus from fellow seekers of the Spirit in the Shalem community and from the long lineage of great mystics in and beyond the Christian tradition who flavor this book in many hidden and manifest ways.

Introduction

So you've been on an intentional spiritual journey a while—maybe for a long while. You've had a variety of hopes and frustrations, experiences and dryness on the way. You've been in and out of churches or other religious communities and centers, praying, learning, questioning, trusting, loving, and leading as you are called, and surprised, by grace.

You find yourself seeking to live and lead in your daily life from a deeper spiritual ground than your surface grasping and fearing ego, or from your thinking mind and senses alone. You may have found that such deeper ground sometimes appears when you're able to let go of your thoughts and ego control and become trustingly present to the radiant Love that *is*. Even if these moments are rare, they may have been enough to give you a dawning sense that this simple but subtle direct openness has major implications not only for your own life but also for our conflicted and confused religious communities and world. You've also probably become aware that the cultivation of such love-fired open presence has a long, rich historical lineage.

If you see yourself somewhere in this spiritual sketch, then you will find some good company and stimulus in this book. What I have said is one very simple way of describing what I see as the contemplative heart of the deepening spiritual journey that today is being reawakened across the world. You will find something in this book that can serve your personal spiritual life, as well as the deeper grounding of your faith and educational communities and other levels of social and Earth living. You will also find help for the fuller formation of your own and others' spiritual leadership (leadership in the sense of opening space for God's Spirit to lead through us in the various contexts of our lives).

Put another way, I want to share with you some practical and theological insights for the deepening spiritual journey, centered on what it is to live with the mind in the heart, and on the overflow of such contemplative openness into our communities and leadership. I purposely have used the term *deepening*, rather than *deeper*, spiritual journey because the Spirit is dropping the bottom out of everyone's self-imposed spiritual floor ever more fully as we're ready and willing for it over our whole lifetime.

Each of us is involved in an ongoing process of conversion to our full being and community in God. The deep spiritual tradition tells us that this process continues through and beyond this life until there is no trace of deluded or willful separation left between us and the Loving One in whose image we are made, or between us and the community of creation.

Because of this ongoing and mysterious journey, I don't see myself as part of some spiritual elite whose members are "deeper" on the spiritual journey than others. I am a fellow sojourner who can share the fruits of my own invited deepening (and resistance to it) as well as what I have learned from others over many years, and I can relate what this experience has done to my way of seeing and being in the world. I do this with a hope and trust that it will connect with your spiritual deepening, since our journeys are being shaped by the same Holy Spirit moving in and among us.

The Spirit's desire, as Jesus taught, is for our deeper *common* life in God through our individual deepening. That deepening is shaped by our graced willingness to embrace the radiant Love shown us through all the fragments of our lives, through all our experiences and options. In that process we find ourselves loosening our grip on anything that would separate us from realizing that Love as the heart of who we truly are and the heart of all creation.

The Influence of Contemplative Tradition

What I have to share is profoundly influenced by what has been given me from the Christian contemplative tradition and its connecting points with other deep contemplative traditions. The neglected gifts of that tradition are tremendously important for our time. In recent years they have spilled over the banks of established contemplative communities and Quaker meetings and flowed into the larger world, often with the help of those communities. Those gifts are becoming leaven for millions of lives today. They also are influencing the ways many churches and seminaries understand and cultivate life lived close to the living Spirit.

The even larger implications of contemplative awareness for our educational institutions, societal living, and Earth care are just beginning to be explored. A contemplative orientation to life can prove to be a vital counterweight to the attraction of fundamentalism across faith lines. It also challenges the sufficiency of any religious or secular views that restrict an appreciation of reality to what the mind can rationally conceive and control. Contemplative awareness provides a door through which the Spirit can take us deeper, freer, and truer, a door through which we can walk beyond any confining room that smothers the Spirit's call to abundant life.

An Outline of the Book

In the first chapter I share my understanding of the nature of contemplative awareness—living with the mind in the heart—as a more direct way of touching deep Reality than our thinking minds can provide. In the second chapter I look at the practices that cultivate contemplative awareness. This is followed by a chapter that explores the range of our possible interior experiences within our times of contemplative openness. Then in the following chapters I turn to contemplative contributions in four major areas:

- Intentional spiritual community in various forms, including in spirituality and monastic centers as well as in cyberspace, with an extended focus on the congregation.
- Broader community in the world, with special sections on contemplative contributions to the reduction of warfare's appeal and the destruction of the Earth, and to the alignment of erotic passion with passion for the divine.
- The nature of spiritual leadership—that is, of being led by the Spirit.
- The formation of the contemplative leader in various contexts besides the congregation and spiritual centers.

In the concluding chapter I introduce a few other contemplative frontiers in our emerging religious communities and world and invite you to bring forward their further exploration.

Experiences of the Deepening Spiritual Journey

Before launching into these chapters, let me mention some movements of the deepening spiritual journey that may be part of your interior landscape, coloring your way of being present to the contemplative arenas that I will spell out. These movements reflect elements of my own experience and those of many others at one time or another. Your own experience may sometimes overlap and sometimes diverge from these, given the marvelously diverse ways we encounter and respond to the Spirit-breezes rising up along life's way.

As the Spirit drops us deeper into our journey, we may well eventually experience three things in one form or another. First, we can feel a certain "sad elation," for lack of a better term. Some illusion or willfulness has dropped away, something we often haven't even been aware of. We are elated by the gift of our new freedom and awareness. At the same time, we're humbled by how blindly kidnapped we were by what now has fallen away as false or inadequate.

Tears may come as a result, both tears of grateful relief for what has now been shown us and of sad humility for having been duped for so long. Such sad elation is not a one-time thing, since there seems to be no end to the illusions that we carry. Just knowing that over time we will be shown more illusions to shed can add a certain humility and openness to our lives. A friend of mine speaks of the realization of such illusions as a kind of gifted repentance, an opportunity to let go of something that has been shown to be too narrow, willful, or false in our lives.

A second impact of our deepening can be disorientation. Maybe God has suddenly been dissolved for us as a demanding judge, or as a reliable parental caretaker, or as a felt loving presence. Maybe everything "spiritual" feels stale and unattractive. We may feel abandoned. If we're Christian, the scriptural passage with which we most identify may be Jesus's cry of abandonment on the cross, or its equivalent in certain Psalms and other writings. Little or nothing of who God was for us still lives. Some underpinning of our previous faith has been taken away. At the same time we may have a sense that, painful as it is, we're being drained of a past orientation that must be let go so that we can be drawn to a fuller sense of divine and human reality. In the meantime, though, we're left hanging, unable to do anything but wait with bare hope in the emptiness, darkness, and confusion of our faith.

On the other hand, we may experience an overwhelming new intimacy with God that challenges our sense of autonomy and of God's clear otherness. We may have difficulty naming God now, because the very naming distances us from the communion we are given. Or we may find ourselves using different names for God, because our past connotations of the word *God* feel too confining. God has burst the straitjacket of past, more limited understandings. Just as we see a new name for God in the Bible when a larger revelation has been received (as in Exodus 3:14), we find ourselves resonating to more inclusive names for the Holy One who appears to us. Our own identity also may be enlarged: our deepest self is felt as part of a larger Self in God.

At times God may seem to so disappear into us, or we into God, that we sense nothing is left. What remains may be a sense that we are just to live our lives in an ordinary way without clear reference to any named Presence. We may want, not to talk about God in any way, but in a sense just to live God by compassionately living who we are day by day. God has become too simple, too ingrained in the fabric of life, to single out.

When God is named in this book, you will find a variety of names given besides "God" in order to invite and name a larger and richer intimacy and reality in our sense of the divine than our conditioned sense of the word *God* may carry for us. As we sense a need in light of our experience to broaden our way of naming the divine Presence, we may find ourselves distanced from spiritual reading that doesn't recognize the transforming depth of this intimacy and its impact on how we see and live in the world and how we name the intimate Presence.

Both kinds of deepening—sad elation and disorienting intimacy—can lead to a third impact: a sense of aloneness. We don't know how to talk clearly about the changes in a way that will make sense to others in our lives. What is happening may be threatening to others who want us to be the way we were for the sake of their own security. Or they simply may not be able to make sense of what's happened to us. We then become more circumspect in speaking to anyone about our evolving spiritual life—we mostly keep it to ourselves, or share it with a spiritual companion/director, although we may feel that even they may not understand.

We may not be able to respond in church and other settings with the same understanding as before. So many things begin to be seen in a different way now, and we may find ourselves called in different directions than in the past. We may no longer be at ease with some religious conversations and actions. Inside we may feel spiritually more of a stranger to others, and even to ourselves. It can be an important time to have a regular and mature spiritual companion/director to whom we can honestly pour out what's going on inside, assuming it is someone we can trust to be patiently open to the grace of what's happening in us, even if they may not understand any better than we do.

If you have any such experience of familiar ground disappearing under your feet, welcome to the deepening spiritual journey! It is a spiritual *journey*, after all. The journey can be full of disorienting surprises and yearnings in us, as we move from the image of God in which we were made toward the full likeness of God (as some early church fathers spoke of the journey).

Perhaps the single most vital thread I have personally found through all of the disruptive movements is one of naked trust. Whatever is taken away from me, or newly given to me, in terms of the content of faith and relationship, I can retain an underlying trust of belonging to a larger gracious Presence who mysteriously pervades and loves what is, through all its volatility.

The Evolving Conversation

Join me now in the spiritual conversation ahead. Join me no matter where you stand in the spectrum of spiritual experience and belief. I will speak from my particular Christian grounding in the way that lives in me at this point in my life, but I trust that grounding can touch whatever is true and yearned for in your own grounding. A contemplative orientation especially makes this possible, for it brings us through and beyond the words of our religious traditions to the shared deep Reality that pre-exists and births the interpretive words.

I can't hear your side of the conversation, but I indeed hope that you will enter the pages ahead with respect for your own experience of spiritual deepening and its impact on your way of being in the world. If something I write isn't understandable or doesn't make sense to you, trust your own experience and just pass on to something I later say that hopefully will make more sense. Threaded through the book is the same overriding theme of deepening awareness and ways of living in radiant Love. In its fullness this is a Spirit-soaked, transforming awareness that radically affects how we see our own and the world's identity and purpose.

As I take us through select facets of the one jewel of the divine Presence, hopefully what I say will have a cumulative effect. What may be opaque to you in looking at one facet may become clearer to you as we shift to another facet. How you understand what I say will relate to your own experience, which may draw out fresh possibilities of what I'm saying that are different from those I articulate.

The conversation will pause at the end of this book, but it will not stop. Every time we're touched in some new way and receive fresh disorientation, insight, and deepening spiritual conversion, the conversation begins anew, as we seek to understand who we are becoming and what we are to do, both alone and together. May the shifts of our journeys lead to our ever fuller participation in the divine heart of reality ever beating in our midst: the mysterious creative Love that is our shared true home.

PART I

*Deepening
Contemplative
Awareness and Practice*

CHAPTER 1

The Gift of Open Awareness: Living with the Mind in the Heart

The Power and Limitation of Our Thinking Minds

I love the mind's words. I love their beauty, their power to reveal meaning, their stimulation of my imagination and playfulness, their facilitation of my practical understanding, their capacity to inspire my will, and the way they enable my communication with others on all kinds of levels. I love to go to the dictionary to look up the Latin, Greek, or other roots of English words that enrich their meaning. I love the way the words of other languages I have studied can give a different feel to reality. I revel in reading scriptural and theological words and the stories of the saints that inspire a fuller sense of spiritual wisdom and risk taking.

Our capacity for words, for thinking and imagination (and the feelings behind them), is an awesome human gift. We spend much of our day attending inner, spoken, and read words and images. However, their very power and familiarity can blind us to their limitation in connecting us to reality as it is. It wasn't until I encountered contemplative awareness that I really came to understand this. Until then I was prone to identify reality with the words

I used to describe it. I saw the "really real" not so much as what I actually experienced but rather as my mental interpretation of the experience. The experience appeared retrievable through my mental interpretation of it, and that interpretation I thought fully carried the substance of the experience itself.

Due to that view, in my early years of contemplative meditation—of open, receptive presence—what I thought really counted most was not so much what happened in the meditation itself but rather my reflection on it afterward. I believed that what my interpretive thinking showed me fully contained what was real in the experience. What happened in the meditation had no real value apart from my reflection upon it. Once I had interpreted my experience, I thought I had captured it with my words. I had acquired a worded, imaged knowledge of it, and I had been tacitly conditioned by most of my formal education to think that this reflective knowledge was the only real knowledge (or at least the *most* real knowledge).

As I matured in my practice with the help of contemplative mentors, it sank into me that my interpretations were my mind's way of trying to translate my firsthand meditation and prayer experience of reality into its mental categories and to latch onto those translations as sufficient comprehension of the experience itself. The urge to do this was enhanced by my security-conscious ego's desire to find names and meanings for experiences that would relieve the anxiety of undefined, uninterpreted experience. In spiritual terms, I wanted clarity about the way God's Spirit was present and calling.

I have come to see that my experience is always larger than my mind's translation of it into words can contain. I still have many words for my experience—that's my mind just being itself. I appreciate and enjoy these mental translations of what's happening, and they can bring to my mind a hint of the divine Presence and calling. But my reflective mind has come to approach experience with hat in hand, much more humble than it once was. I'm aware now that my mind is incapable of exhausting all dimensions of an experience.

If we try to be present in life primarily with our thinking mind (and the sensations and feelings that may precede or follow it), we will likely be satisfied only temporarily with what we're shown. New dimensions of experience come to us that challenge our old interpretations, or new interpretations occur to us about our old experience. Thus, our thinking minds are forever restless, incomplete, searching, haunted in their futile attempt to get the truth down right once and for all, especially spiritual truth. The thirteenth-century mystic Rumi poignantly points to this activity of the mind related to spiritual truth when he says:

> The intellect is that which, constantly, night and day, is agitated and restless from its meditation, effort, and striving to comprehend the Creator—even though the Creator is uncomprehended and incomprehensible. The intellect is like a moth, the Beloved a candle. As much as the moth throws itself upon the candle, it is burned and destroyed. But the moth is that which, however much it suffers harm, burning and pain, cannot do without the candle....Intellect is good and desirable to the extent it brings you to [God's] door.... Know that the intellect's cleverness all belongs to the vestibule. Even if it possesses the knowledge of Plato, it is still outside the palace.[1]

When "getting the truth down right" becomes important to the ego's sense of security, then whatever interpretation of truth has been given us at a particular time may feel ultimate. We will be tempted to hold it tight and unchangeably and want everyone to conform to that understanding. When we succumb to that temptation, especially when we do it as part of a group of like-minded people, we can contribute to the endless tragic ideological wars of which the world painfully knows too much. This isn't to say that some interpretations of truth aren't much more inclusive than others and therefore are particularly worth affirming; but it is different from rigidly asserting that there can be no valid further interpretation, thus objectifying a particular mental interpretation into a universal and unchallengeable truth.

In the current postmodern intellectual climate, such objective frozen interpretation is particularly suspect, as any interpreted "truth" is seen to be at least in part a social construct, related to the language, culture, and circumstances of the interpreter. Such a view need not necessarily lead to a strictly relativistic view of conceptual spiritual assertions, however.[2]

Contemplative Awareness:
Our Special Faculty for Direct Presence

Within us there is a capacity for touching reality more directly than the thinking mind. It is activated when we're willing to let go of the thoughts that come through our mind and to sit in the spacious openness that appears between and behind them.

If you haven't done that before, then when you do you're in for a major discovery. It will be like finding a door that you didn't even know existed. As that door opens, you are led into the reality before you much more directly than your thinking mind can do. Eventually you may find yourself intimately present *within* whatever you see. You are part of it. You know it as it is, just as when you were a small child and your open mind directly entered what you saw and remained there longer than in later years, when your trained interpretive mind quickly took over what you saw on its own terms.

This preinterpretive faculty, our capacity for intuitive "direct awareness," belongs to each of us. We each touch the same substantive reality there. In that direct awareness we share an inclusive sense of community with what is, because we find everyone and everything present and interrelated. When the thinking mind comes into play to interpret that reality through its categories and conditioning, and with the influence of our ego desires for security in that interpretation, the pure contemplative awareness can be splintered into different views and consequent actions. The mind-created differences can be enriching and valuable, but they also can be divisive and can lose touch with the inclusive contemplative awareness that birthed them.

We see an ecstatic and shared form of direct awareness in the Pentecost experience described in the Acts of the Apostles, where Jesus's disciples were touched by the same Presence despite all their linguistic and cultural differences. We sometimes see the division among those same disciples in their later times of disagreement as they tried to interpret spiritual truth and calling from their conditioned minds alone.

The value of precognitive awareness connects with Rumi's invitation: "Out beyond ideas of wrongdoing and rightdoing, there is a field. I'll meet you there. When the soul lies down in that grass, the world is too full to talk about. Ideas, language, even the phrase *each other* doesn't make any sense."[3]

As one of my contemplative mentors once said, "Thoughts are like writing on water."[4] That is, thoughts come from the mind's way of standing outside the water of direct awareness in order to try to understand the water with its own conditioned categories of thought. The mind indeed is able to glean valuable insights on its own terms about whatever it is interpreting; our thought-driven technological accomplishments are one concrete proof of that. But the insights are subject to ever new data that can dissolve or redefine the old understandings. Particular insights can prove insubstantial over time. Their mental categories cannot carry the full reality of the immediate, precognitive awareness of water.

A theologian once said that heresy is whatever reduces spiritual reality to less than it is. Even though the security-conscious dimensions of our minds and human communities like to have an orderly, set understanding of things, the Reality of the beyondness and evolution of spiritual experience is forever opening new understandings of that reality. Revelation is a mystery because no thoughts can ever finally capture its fullness. Mainstream, historically accumulated theological thoughts finally can only imaginatively point us to the depth and trustworthiness of the way mysterious creative divine Love shows itself directly in historical and personal experience as the heart of reality.

The directness of what is exposed of that enlightening Love precedes the thinking mind's commentaries about it. The thinking mind's gifted commentaries are inevitable and valuable as they shape shared faith statements, such as the Nicene Creed, and interpret Scripture and our own experience. But once again: the interpretations are pointers to that which is beyond their final grasp. The creeds have rightly been called symbols of the faith, not the faith itself. The experiential ground of faith's fullness is beyond the mind's grasp. No mental commentary is worthy of worship. That would be idolatry: worship of finite forms. Such idolatry, unfortunately, is rife in the religious and political worlds, to the detriment of the world's peace and of human freedom for further deepening into the largeness of truth.

Scriptural Witness

What we normally experience in the space of direct awareness that precedes our thoughts can be seen as a psychological phenomenon rather than a particularly divinely gifted one. For example, we might sense a simple openness to and intimacy with whatever appears to our consciousness. That is not to be disdained. It is simply what is given and possible at the time, and we can trust that grace is at work behind the scenes of whatever is present. When our awareness is particularly graced, however— that is, when it is directly shaped by loving divine Spirit with a transforming effect on us—it can be called gifted spiritual awareness. Such awareness is the mystical eye of revelation.

Besides the Pentecost experience already mentioned, Scripture shows us such gifted spiritual intuition in many places. For example, we see it in Jesus's life at the time of his baptism, in his wilderness experience, in many of his encounters with people, and in his sense of mission in Jerusalem. This direct spiritual awareness led him to speak to others of the call to reconciled life in divine Love that he was shown. "They were astounded at his teaching, for he taught them as one having authority [i.e., as one having firsthand 'authorship,' 'awareness'], and not as the scribes [i.e., scriptural interpreters removed from gifted firsthand awareness]" (Mark 1:22).

Jesus spoke through metaphors and stories that drew people to the immediacy of life as it is and as it's meant to be in the vast intimacy of the divine Radiance—that is, in the kingdom of God. His firsthand awareness of the Beloved was translated into the thought forms and experiences of his culture, but the intuitive awareness itself transcended his culture. It is to that awareness that he most deeply invites us through his words and acts.

With someone like the great thirteenth-century theologian Thomas Aquinas, the process was reversed. He didn't begin with deeply gifted direct spiritual awareness, he ended with it. After many years focused on the thinking life, during which time he produced profound theological writings, he was suddenly given an overwhelming, ineffable awareness of Reality in God. That graced intuitive awareness so vastly transcended his previous theological thoughts about such Reality that he called his writings mere "straw" by comparison. I wonder if it wasn't from some similar gifted awareness that the twentieth-century Quaker Thomas Kelly could call us to "continually renewed immediacy"—that is, to continually leave ourselves vulnerable to such gifted direct awareness.

Living with the Mind in the Heart

Such realizations point us toward the gifted, intuitive way of knowing the deep Real that is held up by the contemplative tradition. Today this precious contribution of the contemplative tradition is being widely rediscovered and explored after centuries of relative neglect.[5] This way of knowing is connected with what some early church desert elders and their successors over the centuries called living and praying with the mind in the heart. One way of understanding this is to think of it as the process of letting the mind sink into the intuitive spiritual heart's desire for true life in God, including a desire for an immediate awareness of Reality shining in the divine Presence.

We can open ourselves to this way of being present with the help of a variety of practices;[6] however, the fullness of such awareness has always been seen as a divine gift, not as something that we can achieve on our own. Our vulnerable openness in the space between and behind our thoughts can show our willingness for such inspired communion. At the same time, we can be accepting of whatever happens during the practice, trusting that whatever is given is enough for now. It is sufficient just to sit with our trusting, loving desire for real life in the Real One, in whatever different ways beyond our imagining that life may be growing in us over time.

The historical invitation to live with the mind in the heart is phrased in different ways, but they share an overlapping intent. Here is the invitation as stated by Theophan the Recluse, a great nineteenth-century Russian *staretz* (spiritual elder) in the lineage of the desert elders: "The principal thing is to stand with the mind in the heart before God, and to go on standing...unceasingly day and night, until the end of life....Behave as you wish, so long as you learn to stand before God with the mind in the heart."[7]

In terms of Scripture, in which these elders were steeped, they would have read about the importance of living from an open, new heart that "knows" the livingness of God, that realizes Love at the heart of reality.[8] In their constant repetition of the Psalms, they would have absorbed Psalm 51:6: "You desire truth in the inward being; therefore teach me wisdom in my secret heart."

The fourth-century Syrian monk Pseudo-Macarius speaks of not putting all our "trusting hope solely in the scriptures written in ink. For divine grace writes on the 'tables of the heart' (2 Cor 3:3) the laws of the Spirit and the heavenly mysteries....In the heart, the mind abides as well as all the thoughts of the soul and all its hopes."[9] In describing the general view of the early church elders, contemporary Orthodox theologian John Chryssavgis says that "the heart contains the entire *cosmos*, heaven and earth— God Himself....This microcosm or micro-paradise is guarded by the intellect, constantly vigilant and firmly concentrated on the presence of God within the heart."[10]

For some people "mind in heart" imagery might be an easier image for contemplative presence than "open awareness" or similar phrases, even though such mind in heart imagery may be a little misleading unless carefully defined, due to the popular connotations associated with the heart. The heart is more than the seat of the will, feelings, and devotion, which are the qualities we commonly associate with the heart today. The spiritual heart goes beyond these qualities to include another way of knowing reality than that offered by our thinking, figuring-out mind.

The spiritual heart provides a more obscure but substantial loving awareness in God, so obscure to the thinking mind that it could be called a mind of "unknowing" (as we see described in the anonymous contemplative text *The Cloud of Unknowing*). When the thinking mind bathes in the spiritual heart, what the mind then "thinks" is influenced by the heart's purer connectedness with the living Presence.[11]

The mind is a marvelous gift of God, but when the mind is cut off from the spiritual heart it is tempted to idolatry, to the worship of particular interpretations of spiritual truth as the truth itself. As a deceased and beloved colleague of mine, Jerry May, once said, "The mind is a child of the Spirit, but it loves to run away from home." In a sense, the thinking mind cannot be fully at home spiritually, since its very cognitive structure keeps it as an outside observer of direct spiritual awareness. It can create valuable thoughts *about* such awareness, but that is not the same as spiritual awareness itself. The spiritual heart is in more direct and steadier contact with our spiritual home than our thinking mind, and thus we are invited to let our mind be grounded in our spiritual heart, the seat of our contemplative awareness.

A contemplative orientation gives special weight to *open heart listening in the moment*, which then in daily life feeds our figuring-out mind. The mind translates the spiritual heart's awareness into its own reflective categories. It's invaluable to know what the figuring-out mind can tell us about the social, psychological, theological, and practical realities and possibilities of people, spiritual community, and nature. But when it comes to listening for God's obscure Spirit in what's happening, we need to center on an innocent, receptive presence. The mind needs regularly to break up the overly solid and conditioned flow of labeling and interpreting things by repeatedly sinking to the heart with a quality of innocent openness. There it can sit, however briefly, with an open desire to be relinquished to the real Presence and to receive a fresh (or confirmed) sense of deep Reality and what's called for.

It's important to note that these two integrally related faculties of knowing, mind and heart, are not enemies. Each has its gifted place. But they need to have a good marriage and know their place in that marriage. Since the depth of the heart's listening presence usually is much more neglected in the culture's and the church's life, I have put more weight on it in this book.[12]

Further Understanding of Contemplative Awareness

The more direct way of knowing found in contemplative awareness, mind-in-heartedness, allows reality to be itself. It draws us into an awareness of what is happening just as it is, the way it is before our thinking mind clicks in. Faith would add that "what is" is happening within the orbit of divine grace.

Such direct knowing involves, first of all, a deep desire to participate in the flow of God's grace in the living moment. Put another way, I bring a desire to identify the core of my being with the radiant Love who, according to scripture, shapes each of us into a unique image of itself. I also bring a desire to live out of that Love in my daily life. Finally, I bring a trust, or at least a hope, that by suspending attachment to the conditioned concepts and images of my conceptual mind I will be left more vulnerable to the grace at hand that so exceeds what my thinking mind can hold. I will be more available to the movements of the Holy Spirit that animate what is most vital in the living moment. The awareness of deep Reality from my deep soul-self will be awakened.

A long historical stream of spiritual elders make it clear that we cannot bring to this way of knowing that possessive part of ourselves that wants to accumulate knowledge for our self—that wants to collect spiritual things that can enhance our sense of control and security. This tendency toward spiritual materialism is reinforced by powerful commercial and cultural forces that easily leave this overly grasping dimension of self as a pervasive driving force in us.

I know that I need to be empty of this possessive dimension of self as much as possible when I approach this different way of knowing. We find a profound model in Jesus's astonishing release of possessive self-centeredness, climaxed on the cross and described in the great self-emptying hymn in the Letter to the Philippians (5:11). As we come to identify who we most truly are with our deep soul-self in God, we become more capable of relinquishing, or at least of marginalizing, an overly possessive sense of self.[13]

I would add here that our striving ego-self is not intrinsically bad. Its psychic structures are gifts that allow us to function in daily life. It helps us to expediently protect ourselves when that is called for, such as when we get out of the way of an oncoming car. It also helps us to resist oppression, and it enables our functional creativity and caring for others. At its best, it is a good servant of our larger self in God. At its worst, it forgets its place as a servant and becomes the master. Then it loses a sense of our deeper self in God. Ego's energy becomes dispersed in ways that shut off our awareness of its ultimate source in divine Energy and weakens its potential as an instrument of blessing. This is likely followed by a possessively grasping and fearful motivational ground, where we find self-emptying much more difficult.

Cynthia Bourgeault illustrates well the relation of ego and heart when she says: "As you nurture the heart, your ego will begin to relativize of its own accord. It can then do its real job as a useful instrument of manifestation—in the same way a violin lets you manifest the music. But you have come to know that you are not your violin."[14]

Conclusion

If contemplative awareness—mind-in-heartedness, as I have described it—is new to you and you're still a little uncertain about what it means, I encourage you to stay the course. I think you will find it becoming clearer as we go along, especially in the next chapter, where I take up contemplative practices, and in the following one, where I look at the range of things we might come to experience and "know" during our times of open presence. Even with greater intellectual clarity, however, our real understanding will come only through our own firsthand experience with contemplative presence. That will be a more intuitive understanding, one that your thinking mind can trust but only dimly grasp.

For those of you who already are on the contemplative road, I hope that what's ahead will confirm your own contemplative awareness as well as stimulate your sense of its possible contribution to all dimensions of human living.

When contemplative awareness is inspired by the holy breath of God's Spirit reverberating in our spirits, scales fall from our eyes and we are empowered to be more discerning and freer vessels of the creative Love that has moved us. That Love helps to shape our individual and communal future, relentlessly rising up again and again amid the narrowing counterforces in and around us that God's Spirit mysteriously allows and invites to conversion.

CHAPTER 2

Practices for
Open Awareness

Why Take Up a Contemplative Practice?

Let me emphasize at the beginning that any authentic spiritual practice, at least within the mature Christian tradition, is not a way of bringing in an absent divine Presence. Especially in the experience of the contemplative tradition, the divine Presence already *is;* it is the sea in which we swim and that flows inside of us as well. So then why do we take up a spiritual practice?

First, taking up a spiritual practice can be a sign of our desire to trust and live out of the divine Presence, the radiant Love that lies at the heart of our deepest identity and at the heart of all that is. No matter what happens during the time of the practice, if it is grounded in this longing trust, we are inviting Love to grow in our lives, however hidden from our consciousness that action of Love may be.

Second, the practice can be a way of loosening the conditioned view of our ego-dominated consciousness and will. This confused view gives us a sense of overseparateness from the community of creation and communion in God. That sense of over-separateness leads to the overfearing, protecting, and grasping that are the roots of so many of the world's ills.

A spiritual practice can challenge the warped powers and principalities of the world as well as our own illusions and nar-

16

row willfulness. These forces can enthrall us to a life that hides and distorts our true nature and community. An authentic spiritual practice throws down the gauntlet and, in the spirit of Deuteronomy 30:19, says, "Choose life, real life in God; I shun the empty, isolating ways that lead to death." To sustain this choice we need daily practices that counter the ways of death and draw us to the ways of life.

A spiritual practice is aimed at softening us up, making us porous to the living sacred waters of life, to the intimate reality of life as it is in God. We are inviting a vulnerability to whatever we need to realize communion and calling. The practice is a means of disposing ourselves to the grace at hand. It cannot "create" the grace. We can only want to be available in trust to whatever grace would shape in us.

Particular Practices

The particular spiritual practices that we are personally invited to take into our lives are a subject for our listening prayer. There is no one "right" group of practices for everyone, but there is some right set of practices for each of us at any given time in our lives. This chapter will offer in detail a very few practices, one or more of which may help you to appropriate some dimension of the open awareness that I emphasized in the last chapter. I have written about many more contemplatively oriented practices in my previous books, especially in *Living in the Presence*,[1] and many of them are suitable for beginners. Here I describe only a few practices that will likely be most appreciated by people who already are experienced with some form of contemplative prayer.

Some spiritual practices are more for our set-apart times of solitude, while others are ones we thread through our daily work and play, joy and sorrow. Over time particular practices may wear out and be replaced by others that are more suitable. After many years some people may move toward a more seamless presence in the Presence that requires less attention to any particular practice. When we live in challenging circumstances that are not supportive of our sense of spiritual Reality, then we are likely to be most in need of countervailing practices that remind us of who we and the world most truly and deeply *are* in God.

It can be helpful to have a trusted spiritual companion with whom we can probe the kinds of practice called for at a particular time in the context of our evolving spiritual journey, someone who can listen with us over time for the Spirit's movements in our lives. I have described this relationship in several previous books, most recently in *Spiritual Director, Spiritual Companion*.[2] Such intentional companionship is a spiritual practice in itself, to which I will briefly return later in this book.

The Gift of Contemplative Practices from Another Tradition

I personally became most deeply appreciative of contemplative awareness through time spent in 1973 and thereafter with a Tibetan Buddhist high lama, scholar, and meditation master, Tarthang Tulku, Rinpoche. In 1977 I wrote about my experience with him in the introduction to my first book, *Living Simply Through the Day*. That was a period of my life when I was strongly moved to explore further contemplative resources for the spiritual life, and some friends urged me to include the contributions of the Buddhist tradition, as Thomas Merton and other Christian contemplatives had paved the way for doing in the previous several decades.

For the sake of my readers who have never been involved in such an exploration beyond their own Christian or other faith tradition and perhaps have some suspicion of doing so, let me pause here and offer you a hopefully reassuring bridge.

My own belief and experience is that we can learn from whatever is true in other deep spiritual traditions without threat to the integrity of our own. St. Paul, in Philippians 4:8, says, "Fill your minds with whatever is truthful, holy, just, pure, lovely and noble. Be mindful of whatever deserves praise and admiration." The Second Vatican Council's document on non-Christian religions advocated learning what is true and holy in other traditions. My time with Tarthang Tulku, Rinpoche (and with certain other Buddhist teachers since), confirmed the Roman Catholic theologian John Dunne's view, written in that same period, that the spiritual adventure of our time involves a passing over from one religion, culture, and way of life to another and coming back with new insight to our own.[3] Many theologians and monastic contemplatives, along with a great many lay seekers, have done just that in the last half century.

I believe that Christianity cannot hope to be fully catholic, in the broad sense of inclusively embracing of spiritual truth, unless it remains open to consonant truth shown through the generosity of divine grace spread through the experience of people in the world's other deep spiritual traditions. As a Christian, I believe that God's reconciling Spirit in Christ is inviting openness to insights and practices today that expand our horizons in such a way that we find our understanding of Christ, God, and spiritual Reality deepened and widened. This invitation has been offered and positively responded to by many people at various times in church history. Today, however, is distinguished by an unprecedented availability of extensive knowledge related to all other deep spiritual traditions.

The Backdrop of Contemplative Theology

I believe that the contemplative strands of the deep spiritual traditions overlap, especially in their recognition of the intimate "interwovenness" of people, creation, and the divine. I want to offer here one way of looking at that interwovenness from a Christian contemplative perspective. A sense of such mutual indwelling is a mental backdrop for contemplative practices. (If you don't need a theological perspective here, you can skip this section and proceed to the next one.)

If God is dynamically One, as Scripture declares over and over in different ways, then all truth flows from the same divine Source. In all humility, we need to recognize that none of us can absorb all the particular spiritual revelations that have been given to humankind. Because of that limitation, we could well say that only God can be fully catholic. However, we don't need to absorb all of them. If God is an integral unity and cannot be divided into parts, then God appears in divine Wholeness in all concrete appearances (perhaps obliquely analogous to a hologram). But we cannot fully comprehend that wholeness with our limited minds. Along the way of our journey, the Holy One is forever unfolding more enlightened Love that draws us further into the realization of that loving Wholeness. We can remain open to whatever way the one radiant Love may be showing itself at a given time and place.

Whatever we have been given and have embraced of spiritual truth is enough, until we are invited to further encounter. Our protective, equilibrium-oriented psyches are tempted to freeze the received truth at some point and not risk the disorientation of what else God's living Spirit would show us for our further transformation and the world's good. Our yearning spiritual heart trusts, however, that any disorientation is simply the small price we pay for growing deeper into our true being and calling.

Scripture itself is full of such challenging invitations to larger life in God. Jesus was particularly challenging to this end. He shows us God's loving, bearing, transforming Presence alive in the world beyond what people had imagined. He points us to the mysterious, intimate, yet vast divine Reality that is the inspiring heart of creation. We can see shining in him the trustworthy One who underlies and outlasts the ceaseless changes, dark nights, and joys of life, and who draws us to a deeper communion and common good.

One contribution of certain contemplative practices found beyond the formal Christian tradition is the way they can help reinforce our awareness of the incredible intimacy of life. This awareness counters the frequently built-in dualism—the over-separation of self, creation, and God from one another—that is found in the assumptions of much noncontemplatively oriented Christian (as well as Jewish and Islamic) theology and piety. This dualism can impede our appreciation of the full intimacy that leads to the abundance of life in God that Jesus knew and would have us realize.

Much that I say in this book reflects this intimate understanding of the divine-human relationship. For further clarification, let me offer another "word window" through which to look at who we are in relation to God and creation. A key word here is *nondualism*; that is, we can't finally speak of ourselves without also speaking of what seems "other" than ourselves—God and creation. They are not the same, and yet all three belong to one another. They are not one, nor are they separate. We cannot authentically speak of one without implying the other. At the heart of our deep human identity we don't find some ultimately autonomous being. We find what Genesis 1:27 calls a distinctive image-reflection-mirror of the divine Reality.

My "I" is seen to be integrally connected with the divine "I Am" (God's revealed name to Moses in Exodus 3:14). As the theologian Raimon Panikkar has said,[4] we could call the otherness of that divine "I" by another name: "Thou." But that otherness is not alien to me; it is the depth dimension, the not-fully-known reality of who I truly am.

The rest of creation is intimately involved in this larger Reality as well. Thus, I cannot realize the fullness of "I" without including the larger "I" of God, God both beyond creation and God the ongoing breath of creation. All of Reality thus is mirrored in my being, as my being is mirrored in the rest of Reality. I am a distinctive image, a unique expression, of God's Presence in creation. The multiple dimensions of God reflected in the Christian view of the Holy Trinity reflect such an irreducible mutuality: God is One, Holy, Whole, yet in trinitarian expression, God is unity in diversity. As St. Augustine and others have said, we share in that Reality. Another key word increasingly used in Christian contemplatively oriented theology today to express such intimate nondualism is *panentheism*.[5]

Such an understanding points to the incredible loving intimacy that the contemplative tradition especially holds up as the pinnacle of spiritual awareness. I find that it reflects many of the daily yearnings in me: for intimate physical and spiritual communion and yet for personal distinctiveness, for community and for solitude, for merger and for separation, for sacrifice and for creative assertion, for self-emptied receptive presence and for spontaneous action.

When I have a theological framework of nondualism for these different interior movements, I am able to see their connectedness rather than their competitiveness. I see their need for one another, their mutual dance in the unfolding of abundance. This view helps to free me from an overblown individualism (so cultivated in our culture) that can leave me more isolated, confused, alien, controlling, and impoverished in my view of reality.

Such a panentheistic view (not a "pantheist" view; see note 5) also can help to free me from a sense of God as an oppressive "Other," a reality not part of my very being, a distant imperial figure who does not shape me out of his own loving energy. As a Christian, a sense of belonging to the vast-intimate mystical Body of Christ becomes one image for countering this debilitating sense of God and self.

The Body of Christ speaks to me of the graced awareness that reveals our integral mutual belonging and freedom beyond our confused and sometimes willful brokenness. We are all insiders of the whole of Reality together. Our ongoing journey reveals our own evolving place in that living Body day by day. Our slowly transformed awareness reveals all life in God and God in all of life, which is a nondualistic description of deep Reality as many great contemplatives have known it.

Relating to Different Contemplative Traditions

Let me say a little more now about the contemplative strands beyond the Christian tradition and more specifically about my own experience with the contemplative practices that I learned from Tarthang Tulku, Rinpoche. These are practices that I have found can supplement Christian contemplative practices that expose an intimate nondual Reality. These practices can become means of further receptivity to the wondrous radiant Love that melts any rigid, narrow boundaries of our overdefining minds and our oversecuring egos.

I am not implying that I have found all major world faith traditions to be the same. They can be very different in their practices, interpretations of reality, and emphases, even as I sense a precious overlap, especially in their moral and contemplative dimensions. There also can be very different emphases and tensions *within* each tradition—no tradition is monolithic. Each tradition also includes its own shadow side (just as does every culture and individual), a side that loses the wondrous, liberating love and falls into fear, rigidity, exploitation, domination, overexclusiveness, and destructiveness of the human spirit. Our human condition does not permit consistent purity within any tradition;

thus, we find the need for ongoing discernment in what we embrace and for advocacy of ongoing needed reformation.

Nonetheless, despite all the haze that keeps reappearing, we find a certain loving radiance shining through each deep spiritual tradition in its own way, and we see tested paths of potential liberation from our unnecessary suffering and delusion. I believe, though, that whatever is true in each tradition ultimately derives from the same shimmering Wellspring of truth, and therefore in the depth of each tradition we can hope to glimpse something of that life-giving truth.

We can share with others what our own tradition and personal awareness have shown us of that deep Reality. Jesus's followers are told to share the Good News that has touched them as the best news we have to share with others. Christians can do this in a way that remains open to hearing the best news that others have received. We don't need to come up with some inclusive religious synthesis. However, we can be open for the Spirit to enlarge our sense of spiritual Reality in these encounters. We can sense (with Raimon Panikkar) that we are part of an intrafaith dialogue, not just an interfaith one. We don't just relate as outsiders to one another: we relate as insiders, with the same underlying human limitations, possibilities, and deep spiritual yearning.

When I was meditating ten hours a day for nearly two months in my first learning time with Tarthang Tulku, Rinpoche, I would read from the Gospels almost every night. The effect of the day's practices sparked many fresh senses of Jesus's words and acts. Sometimes I felt I could touch the hem of the consciousness out of which his words and acts flowed. Indeed, I came to feel that consciousness to be the heart of my desire in praying with scripture: wanting to be as open to the Spirit as Jesus was, wanting to share something of the same Spirit-soaked consciousness from which he lived and invited us to live, wanting to be inside his spirit as it was in God's Spirit.

Perhaps this is what Isaac of Syria in the sixth century had in mind when he advocated reading the spaces between the words of scripture, as well as the words. Reading the spaces, to me, is living into the spacious divine Ground out of which the words at their purest flowed. The practices of the Tibetan Buddhist tradition to which I was exposed, so far removed historically from any significant contact with the Christian tradition, invited me into that open spaciousness between the words, behind the words, before the words. There, perhaps in graced moments, is where we most directly taste the Wellspring of the "mind of Christ."

I'm reminded of Simone Weil's words to the effect that if Christ is the truth, then wherever the truth is, Christ can't be far away. We touch the truth of reality as it is in spacious open awareness, which our thinking minds then translate into words that allow us to share something of what is beyond words with others. When our shared words draw others to that same openhearted awareness in themselves, then we find ourselves together in the foundational spiritual home where authentic words and actions come from.

Select Practices

In my teaching over the years, besides offering traditional Christian contemplative practices I have adapted certain contemplative practices from other traditions to a specifically Christian contemplative context. The exercises often have led people to a more available and direct presence to reality as it is in the divine radiance, before the conditioning of self-images and thinking click in.

The first three practices I have selected to describe here are limited to ones that directly assist our suspension of self-image (which I will explain later) as a means of cultivating contemplative awareness. They are partly drawn from my experience with Tarthang Tulku, Rinpoche, but I do not claim that they represent the subtlety of his own understanding. I can simply offer what I have perceived from these exercises, adapted to a Christian context. At times they include his particular metaphorical vocabulary for certain processes of our consciousness designed to keep them as concrete as possible.

I have added two more practices drawn from the Christian tradition. The first is praying with classical Christian icons, approached in a way that also can lead to a suspension of controlling self-image and to a cultivation of open awareness. However, this practice also holds up a very personal relational context of people and God so emphasized in the Christian tradition. The second practice, a movement meditation that also can lead to a suspension of self-image, is an example of how the body's movements can draw together all dimensions of our being in an expression of ecstatic open presence.

Contemplatively oriented practices such as *Centering Prayer* (popularized by the Cistercian monks Basil Pennington, Thomas Keating, and others) and *Christian meditation* (of which the Benedictine monks John Main and Laurence Freeman have been proponents) have been helpful in introducing thousands of people to a way of being directly and vulnerably present in God's loving Presence, behind and through all the thoughts that emerge. The exercises in this chapter will complement those and other popular practices. They will offer more direct, careful attention to releasing the skewing power of self-image and the observer in our minds. These practices might aid in disposing us more fully and steadily to an intimate presence in reality as it *is*, just as it is.

In the contemplative tradition, full, transforming communion is a pure gift; it's not something that we can make happen. In the deep contemplative tradition, such communion is seen as a gift that already exists, but it has not yet been realized in its empowered fullness. In this view we always have been "part" of

God, having been made of God's Spirit-energy. The experiential recognition of this communion (or union, in the fullness of communion) and its transforming effects in our lives are by grace given to us over time, often just through brief glimpses. The various dimensions of communion are described with particular depth in the poetry and commentaries of John of the Cross and in the writings of his spiritual friend, Teresa of Avila, among others in the Christian tradition.

I take this process of spiritual deepening to be the central meaning of the early church fathers' words about life being a movement from the image to the full likeness of God. Some of the early church fathers called this process *theosis*, "deification," the process of realizing our gifted godly nature, our sharing in the divine movement of Love. The Eastern Orthodox churches put great emphasis on this sense of ultimate human purpose, grounded in scriptural texts and in the experience of mystical saints.[6] Many Western churches would come closest to expressing this process in the word *sanctification*, our gifted evolution toward holiness: wholeness of life in God.

Letting Go of Self-Images

The deepening spiritual journey moving us toward wholeness of life in God includes an ongoing process of self-emptying —emptying of whatever comes between us and our true being in God. One practical dimension of self-emptying is our willingness to let go of our ultimate identification with *any* image we have of ourselves, good or bad. This goes against the grain of my psychological conditioning, where I was taught to try and replace conditioned negative self-images with positive ones. On a psychological level this can make practical sense; but I learned long ago that it doesn't make spiritual sense.

In the practices Tarthang Tulku, Rinpoche taught related to self-images, I experienced how these images, positive and negative, can be hidden screens in us through which our experience is interpreted. They can shape many of our responses in a way that subtly sustains a self-referencing, limiting, and skewed view of Reality. The second and third exercises later in this chapter give special attention to relinquishing our attachment to self-images, although in my experience all contemplative practices indirectly assist such letting go.

Self-images are necessary on the functional level of our lives. They are part of our practical psychic orientation for daily living. Self-images become problematic when they come to fully define and control our sense of who we really are. St. Paul says that who we really are "is hidden with Christ in God" (Col 3:3). In other words, we are much more than our little conscious self-images say that we are. If we share the divine DNA as a unique image of God, then our full identity is far vaster than our minds can ever grasp. In the fullness of who we are we belong, not to an ultimately separate self, but to the eternal deep Reality we call God. As I have said in different words before, we are a special shaping of God's radiant Love-energy. Thus, that Spirit-energy lives in us, however hidden it may be, just as it lives beyond us.

If we can trust God's integral involvement in our hidden true identity, then it will be easier for us fearlessly to suspend our conditioned, possessive self-images. We realize that we exist beyond any self-image. We do not disappear when our self-images dissolve. We then can be more openly receptive to the way deep Reality shows itself on its own terms, just as it is, before the conditioning effects of self-image set in.

An Overview of the Practices

As I mentioned earlier, if you have no exposure to contemplative practices, you need to realize that those given here are not normally exercises for beginners, although you may still find them helpful. I want to offer you the gist of what I have come to see as certain often missing, subtle dimensions of practice and understanding in the renewal of contemplative awareness in the Christian tradition today. I have added my own theological commentary at times.

Much of the first three exercises involves a careful psychological process aimed at showing us reality as we become aware of it before our interpreting minds and self-images click in. In the way we're given to intuitively know reality then, what we know is not so skewed by our conditioned thinking and our self-referencing and overly separated sense of self (i.e., more separated from the rest of creation and from God than we really are). We then are often more susceptible to receiving whatever real grace is meant for us at the time.

It's worth noting that any method of meditation or prayer can be seen to begin with some psychological process, a mental way of opening ourselves beyond the confines of our little selves, but spiritually our intent is not psychological curiosity or controlling manipulation. Our intent is to open ourselves to reality as it is. In our faith, this includes a trust that true reality is suffused by radiant divine loving Presence.

The first three exercises could be called teaching exercises, in the sense that they are more carefully guided toward a particular quality of awareness than the more directly prayerful exercises, which are designed to give you a simple starter toward open presence in the Presence, leaving you available for the Spirit's unforeseen movements. These teaching exercises are only meant for very occasional practice, as they may help us to let go of interior distancing tendencies that can build up in us through much cultural reinforcement and can be barriers to realizing a more directly open, intimate presence. The two practices that follow these three teaching exercises are more directly aimed at prayerful presence. They connect with many other more widely used practices for open presence to God.

The three teaching practices can be disorienting in their uncovering of a different way of seeing and being present in reality than we're used to. They may bring us to the edge of a larger consciousness that we don't quite comprehend but that seems to free us for a fresh awareness not bound to our normal hard identification with self-images and thoughts.

You may find just one of these practices to be of value for you now. Over time you may find yourself changing the words and adapting the practices to your own understanding and way. None of them may connect with where you are, in which case you can simply close this door and open whatever other door of practice and exploration is given you at this point in your life. You do not need to understand or use these particular practices in order to understand what is written in the following chapters.

EXERCISE 1: OPEN AWARENESS BEFORE AND THROUGH OUR THOUGHTS

How can we retain some degree of open presence in the larger gracious Presence when our minds are so easily divided from that presence through identification with the myriad thoughts that bombard us every minute? How can we extend that openness to divine Love's presence to the spaces between our thoughts?

This exercise can help us to remain available to the larger Presence right through our thoughts and the open spaces between them. Given our broken human condition, we no doubt will never remain continuously available. Our minds are like a flawed electrical connection to a lamp that sometimes is able to let in the light, and sometimes isn't. This exercise might at least invite the holy light to shine through our consciousness a little more often, so that we don't miss the grace at hand quite so much. We might taste a little more freedom for our Spirit-soaked soul to suffuse and guide our thoughts and wills. The process of the exercise also will likely help us become a little better acquainted with the operation of our mind moment by moment as it affects our awareness.

Ideally, you could record the written guidance of this and the other exercises here so that you could just listen to them rather than having to continually return to reading their steps. Alternatively, you could have someone else read them to you and, in a group practice, to any others who might be with you. The suggested amounts of time are the minimum I would advise. My occasional commentaries that go beyond the instructions for the exercises can be skipped until after the exercises are done.

1. Take a slow, deep breath, relax, and close your eyes. Open your desire to live from your deep soul-self in God, right through everything in your life. Be open for the way this exercise might leave your presence in God less eclipsed by particular things registering in your mind, more available to the stream of grace running behind and through whatever appears in your mind.

2. Begin counting absolutely everything that appears in your mind. This includes thoughts, images, sensations, desires, and feelings. Let your mind be the way it normally is, except for this: simply count whatever registers and immediately, gently let it go, without being kidnapped by anything that appears. If something reappears, count it again. Take about five minutes for this step, then take another deep breath and relax a minute.

3. Close your eyes again. This time shift your emphasis to remaining in the spaciousness *between* your thoughts. As any thought, image, sensation, desire, or feeling begins to rise, note (but don't count) it and immediately let it pass

by as you remain steadily in the open spaciousness. If you do notice yourself dwelling on the content of something that appears, gently let it fade into the spaciousness. Just settle into a simple, open, steady spacious presence. After about five minutes, take a slow breath again and relax a moment. You might notice that the spaciousness is not an empty nothing. It is an inclusive consciousness, a "full-emptiness," an infinite horizon.

4. Close your eyes once again. For a final period of at least ten minutes, instead of counting or briefly noting what appears, see each appearance (of a thought, image, sensation, desire, or feeling) as a particular shaping of that energy-filled spaciousness out of which it arises. You might sense each one as a vibrant bubble rising up and retaining its transparency to the atmosphere out of which it arises. Each appearance can be seen as a unique shaping of the pregnant spaciousness out of which everything is born. Thus, you can notice a great intimacy between what appears and the spaciousness out of which it appears.

5. Once you become familiar with this way of attending whatever shows itself, you can bring your faith to bear and for a few minutes gently extend this intimacy to the Gracious One whose Spirit-energy pervades the ever-pregnant spaciousness and whose ebullience inspires the shaping of endless forms.

6. For a few more minutes, see what it's like to sense *yourself* as part of this divine economy. You also are a unique shaping of God's Spirit, created in the image of God. You are created to be a unique transparency of loving light in the world. You are not an opaque and totally separate entity. You are part of God's Wholeness. Your full home is not in yourself separately; it is in your deep being in God.

7. Now take a long, slow breath and relax. That is the end of the practice.

DISCERNMENT OF SPIRITS

Let me briefly add here something about discernment of spirits, which could relate to any practice. As you look back over that practice time, you may have sensed some shapings of your thoughts and feelings that are more remotely related to the Spirit's effusions—shapings that come from the magnetic pull of our separateness, our physical and mental desires for such things as security, bodily care, and achievement. The thoughts and feelings shaped by such expedient needs and self-centered wants can be distinguished from those that more directly draw us to the larger gracious Presence, in terms of both communion and invited action.

Distinguishing these different seedbeds for the things that rise in our consciousness leads us into the process of discernment of spirits. This process, spelled out by St. Ignatius of Loyola, for example, historically also would notice a third source of what comes to us beyond Spirit and ego—the alien but tempting seedbed of evil. Discernment of spirits has been written about extensively, and I won't go into that large subject here.[7]

Whether discernment of spirits is a conscious or unconscious process in us, we're involved in such discernment every day, as we choose which risings in us to heed and which to ignore. The first exercise I have described, among other things, hopefully can help condition us to be freer to relinquish whatever rises in us that does not shine with Love's light, freer not to be kidnapped and dragged around by just anything that appears.

Isaac of Syria in the early church said that the myriad thoughts that rose in him felt like being bitten by myriad mosquitoes. We need practice in the freedom not to scratch every bite that comes along, practice in remaining openly aware behind and between our thoughts, where we sit in the divine Spirit's spacious seedbed. There we can find ourselves at home, confidently present, alert, at ease, and available to the shinings of the Spirit in us.

From that vantage point, over time we may come to see the transparency of what appears in our consciousness to God's radiant Love. We can find that whatever appears need not take us away from that radiance. The appearances themselves can carry something of that divine creative, healing, transforming energy, however hidden or distorted that may be. Eventually we may become more sensitive to those appearances that carry personal invitations for us: invitations to further appreciate divine-human-earth communion or to manifest love in the world in some form.

EXERCISE 2: RELINQUISHING THE OBSERVING EYE OF SELF-IMAGE

Someone once told me that he noticed a different quality of presence in a singer he had heard in performance when she shifted from a complete participation in her singing and environment to a self-conscious sense of presence that drew her away from her flowing, innocent presence within what was happening. An interior observer split off from her integral presence and took center stage. Such an observer emerges every time we step outside the immediacy of what's happening in order to safeguard self-image and relate to the world accordingly. When the observer arises, the singer might suddenly become afraid of making a mistake or wanting to gain approval, or she might worry about the way she looks.

This observer is the eye of our ego-self-image. When we try to experience our self-image, the observer is the first thing we encounter. Beyond our sense of the observer, our experience of self-image is likely to be only a vague sensing of some hidden, self-referencing conditioning power in us. We will tend to identify with the observer as "me" in a more intimate sense than with its more subtle background: self-image. I will return more specifically to self-image in the next exercise. Right now, let's see what happens when we notice the "egoic" observer:

1. Close your eyes and relax. Be in touch with your ultimate intent in doing this exercise, an intent that could be

worded as your desire to openly participate as fully as possible in what is, just as it is, in God.

2. See if you sense an observer of what's happening inside your mind. When you do, look directly at this phenomenon with great energy, until it dissolves completely for a while. If this happens, you may realize a more pure, open, non-self-centered quality of awareness. Remain in that awareness as long as you can.

3. You might notice an observer of the observer arising. If so, energetically look directly at it until it dissolves, and at any others that may arise, so that you are continually returning to simple, open awareness as much as possible. Don't judge the observers that rise, just energetically look through them until they dissolve of their own insubstantiality. That dissolution leaves you more directly present in whatever appears, and in the spaces between whatever appears. You can be very light with the observers, not giving them any substance—just very simply let them go again and again as they appear. Continue doing this for at least ten minutes.

4. Take a few slow, deep breaths and rest for several minutes, and then return to noticing the observer for another ten minutes. This time ask yourself: Where does the observer come from? Don't think about an answer, but try to directly experience where it comes from; be directly present as it arises.

This exercise can show us that the egoic spectator is not a steady presence. It is insubstantial in itself, even though we will notice how we can cling to it as the ultimate "me." When it is suspended, we find that we are more directly within the flow of life, within what's happening now, within the Reality of what is, just as it is. We participate in a living awareness that does not require the distancing eye of an observer. We may then experience a quality of intuitive awareness from the inside of what is, because there is no self-referencing observer or thought keeping us outside.

We have not lost our real self in this process. We have simply let go of our ultimate identity with the insubstantial observing eye of self-image. In its place is a non-self-referential quality of presence. We then find ourselves intimately connected with whatever appears, just as it is. We are part of a larger matrix of vibrant appearances, moment by moment. In our background faith, we may sense that we're left more calmly vulnerable to the radiant loving energy of the Holy One, who wondrously animates and sustains that matrix moment by moment, as part of the interwoven communion of creation.

This exercise may be the most difficult to absorb of all the ones in this book. If you've found a hint of value in it, then you may want to repeat it a few times and see what further value it may show. Exercise 3 may help to bring further light to it. If the exercise is totally opaque to you, then I would advise not worrying about it and moving on. The intended value of this practice for contemplative awareness will come through to you through some other means. There's nothing essential about this particular way.

EXERCISE 3: OPEN PRESENCE THROUGH A MIRROR

When we look at ourselves in a mirror, what do we see? Who is that figure? How do I look? How do I feel about it? What mental self-images are shaping what I see? How do others feel about what I see? What can I do about it?

Looking at yourself in a mirror can involve a powerful temptation to identify these physical and mental dimensions of self-image, not just as the surface of your self, but as the real "you," the real center of your reality that needs all kinds of special attention. This is especially true in a society (and a church as it reflects the society) that puts much weight on the centrality of the individual.

This exercise offers a different approach to the self-image. It can lead us to a participation in reality beyond any image of ourselves, where we might realize our fuller identity and belonging in God through whatever is happening in the moment. This exercise can involve a disorienting, surprising, and revealing awareness, so you might want to ensure that you have someone with whom you could share your experience soon after as you might sense the need, such as a spiritual director, before undertaking it for more than a few minutes. Spend at least half an hour, and preferably an hour, on this exercise.

1. Seat yourself about two feet away from a mirror large enough to see your whole face, where enough light falls on the mirror to light up the face you see in the mirror.

2. Close your eyes, and open your willingness to let yourself be stilled and opened to the way reality presents itself, trusting in Love's encompassing presence through whatever appears.

3. Open your eyes, and instead of grasping for something outside you in the mirror with your eyes, let yourself be seen by the eyes in the mirror. Thus, "you" are not looking at the image in the mirror; rather, the image in the mirror is looking at you. Your attention is interior: you're not grasping for something beyond you, you're letting yourself be seen.

4. Let that gaze from the mirror be so energetic that it melts any sense of an internal observer singling out a self-image or a "mirror image." Without that observer defining and distancing you, your awareness can find itself inside whatever appears. Then many vivid phenomena may appear over time in the mirror, such as your face

being replaced by faces of people known and unknown to you or by light or by scenes of various kinds.

5. Settle into an even, confident-in-God presence through whatever happens, including through times when nothing seems to happen (which may be most or all of the time). Don't try to make anything happen or to suppress anything. If a distancing observer appears in your mind, let it gently dissolve and just return to being in what's happening, with all separating self-definition suspended.

6. When you end you may want to do some descriptive journal keeping for a few minutes, descriptive in the sense of not trying to interpret what happened, but just simply describing whatever you remember that occurred. At some point you may want to see what it's like to do this writing with no possessive pronouns, no "my" or "I" words that single you out, so that you can simply let what was there show itself as part of a happening before any self-definition appears. Then you are letting what is there be just what it is, a reality in which you belong, in which you can be present without separating self-consciousness.

We all know times when we are so completely into what's happening that we have forgotten ourselves; we have not carved out a separate self in our consciousness, even though we are a distinctive part of what's happening. In this exercise we're inviting such intimate, coinherent presence. That quality of unselfconscious awareness carries its own intuitive knowledge of reality.

You can practice letting that obscure-to-the-mind knowing be sufficient for now, without having to attach it to an overly separate image of self and without trying to possess it with your rational interpretations. You might taste a great simplicity in such sufficiency. There are many times, of course, when we need our rational interpretations in life, but it can be liberating to realize that this can be a discerned choice rather than a necessity. There is another more direct way of knowing reality that sometimes is sufficient and preferable.

I have sensed many of the phenomena appearing in the mirror as projections of my own psyche. This has taught me that much that I see in life is really seeing the workings of my mind shaping the world in my mind's image instead of seeing what is really there. As these phenomena wear themselves out in the time of this practice, however, I sometimes seem to become briefly more in touch with what really is present, beyond the dominant overlay of my projections. What is shown as really present can transcend the normal conditioned mental boundaries of time and space.

In a spiritual sense, in graced moments I sense that I am more spontaneously present and available in what is. I'm no longer relating a conditioned image of self to an image of creation and to an image of God, with all the distortions and limitations of such a mentally categorized relationship. I'm present in reality, in creation, in God, before this naming, this categorizing, begins. I am one part of a larger wholeness. I am inside that wholeness, which is vibrant with life and streaming from a marvelous Wellspring. I am inside a larger movement of interwoven forms, beauty, love, and wonder, as well as inside the tear in the weave in whatever shows itself as disrupting or missing this shared dance.

At its purest and most graced, as our interpreting mind might later word it, this being part of what is would take the form of God's gift of transforming communion. Then a person is fully alive in Love, completely at Home. I say "a person" rather than "I" because I am not personally aware of having been touched by more than the hem of that loving communion. However, that touch has left me with a deep trust that beneath any sense of complete separateness created by our categorizing minds, we all live within a communing union, and we are meant to realize at least the glimmer of that transforming fullness in this life. Its resonance in us may be very plain—a simple awareness with no affective dimension—or it may be deeply felt.

To return to the mirror exercise, when I am fully in it I no longer seek to possess separately any dimension of what I see, because I have suspended the self-image that is my interior "collector." I realize that I am part of what I see. Spiritually speaking, my "I" at its heart is made of the same Love-energy as everything else I see (however misused it might be in the mysterious freedom that is part of my "I"). I am a unique mirroring of a larger whole, welling up from the divine Wellspring, and it is for me to live out my distinctive part of that whole. I might put a twist on the meaning of St. Paul's words (2 Cor 6:10) and say that I realize that I have nothing, yet I possess all things; that is, I possess nothing ultimately separate from the whole. Being part of the whole, however, everything is available to me. God is the pulsing heart of the whole, beating in me and through me—and you.

EXERCISE 4: SEEING AS WE ARE SEEN

We can sit before another kind of mirror: a classical icon with the full face of Christ or Mary (or another holy figure) gazing at us. This has been part of my practice for many years. In the center of my prayer space at home is an icon called the Sinai Christ, one of the oldest extant icons (sixth century), the original of which I once was privileged to see hanging in the monastery of St. Catherine at the foot of Mount Sinai. A reproduction of this icon has become available now (e.g., through the Icon and Book Service in Washington, D.C.). Many different icons are available today, and you may already have one. For prayer, it is helpful to find one to which you feel personally drawn and, probably, in which the eyes of the icon are looking directly at you.[8] The description of this exercise will assume that you are using an icon of Christ; you can adjust the words for any other holy figure you may have before you.

1. Sit before the icon, perhaps with a lit candle in front of it as a reminder of the living Presence. Be in touch with your desire for this icon to be a transparency for God's enlivening Spirit in Christ. If your mind or body is restless, you might take a few slow, deep breaths or very slowly move your arms up and down or whatever else might help your mind and body to be calmed and receptive.

2. Let your eyes settle in Christ's eyes and remain there as long as you're moved to remain, perhaps for twenty minutes or longer. Rather than trying to know and possess something with your rational mind, simply sit with a willing, innocent openness and let yourself be known by the Gracious One through the icon. You might recall Psalm 139's confidence that we are known and loved through and through.

3. Close your eyes but retain a sense of the image alive inside you.

4. Such a way of being present can free an intimacy beyond the telling. The distance between you and the gracious Knower can collapse. Christ's knowing and compassionate gaze can penetrate and melt layers of defense, willfulness, and illusion. You're shown up as you are. You see as you are seen.

Based on my experience with the Sinai Christ icon, a spontaneous repentance may take place, an empowered release of what is seen in me that needs to be relinquished. That becomes possible because the gaze shows me an unchangeable Love at the bottom of my nature, so there is no need for a protective stance. In graced times the Love encompasses and removes what is seen that obscures my true being in Love. What is left after that liberation is a sense of belonging to that Love, a spontaneous freedom to live in and from that Love.

As I move into life after such a time of prayer, I try to feather out its showings into the following hours by briefly recalling them at times, mentally or in my journal. If nothing showed itself during the time beyond my desire for fuller life in God, then I bring that desire forward into the day. Even when the deep, central Reality shown in that meditation time is buried in my forgetfulness through the activities of the day, I trust that it is only a hair's breadth away from my awareness, however thick that hair may be at a given time. When I am enabled to recall the radiant Love at the center of reality, that awareness provides a perspective and compass for my activities in the moment. I am more able to live out of that Love, however faintly. I realize who I truly am in God: a unique icon, an image of the invisible One, through whom God loves, bears, and enjoys the world.

EXERCISE 5: MOVING AS WE ARE MOVED

Moving our bodies in prayer is a practice found in all deep spiritual traditions. It may take such forms as raised or clasping hands, swaying, walking, clapping, kneeling, prostrating, and dancing. We could also include singing and chanting, to the extent that they involve the sustained vibration of our vocal chords, and we could add ways of breathing. I want to offer one particular movement practice here.[9] After that I will speak of certain other forms of movement meditation.

The classical contemplative way usually is associated today with the cultivation of an open presence through silent, still attentiveness. The ecstatic way today is associated with a cultivation of a vulnerable presence for the Holy Spirit through expressive pleading and praise, passionate singing, bodily movement and willingness for ecstatic phenomena, such as speaking in tongues and prophecy. I often use the image of calm, clear water for the quality of presence sought by many contemplatives. For people living out a more ecstatically oriented way, I use the image of sparkling, carbonated water. Both hold in common a desire for direct presence to God in the moment.

The specific practice of movement meditation that I will describe here provides an opportunity for silent and expressive forms of presence to thrive together as they may be called forth. I have offered this practice for groups in prayer together, but its basic steps can be practiced alone. In a group I have often offered it in the context of a silent retreat.

1. Begin in silence (in a spacious circle if you are in a group). Be in touch with your desire to be present in God, with all that you are: your body, mind, feelings, will, and intuitive spiritual heart.

2. Play some music that can draw you to move your body and that will last for at least twenty minutes (twice that if you're very ready and willing). Probably the music will best be a simple instrumental piece (or mixture of pieces) that doesn't draw attention to itself but draws you to the Presence. It doesn't have to be specifically religious music, although you might prefer that. One CD that I have often used is the modern piano music of Michael Gettel called "San Juan Suite" (vol. 1). But there is an infinite variety of possibilities, depending on what best involves your whole self. In a group I have found that no particular musical selection is ideal for everyone, but most people are able to find whatever I have used to be good enough for the purpose of the meditation.

3. Move as you may be moved through the music by the Spirit, slow movements or fast, in place or moving around, flowing childlike, unselfconsciously, intimately cocreating motion (and sound as well if you're so moved)—your spirit alive in God's Spirit. If you sense your mind trying to autonomously move your body, you might release that contrivance of your mind by sensing

yourself moving from the center of your body where God's Spirit and your spirit spontaneously flow together. The more unselfconscious you become, the more directly given to God you become, until there is little or nothing left of "you" that is acting separately. As this happens, you might find your separating self-images dissolving, at least sporadically. Then you may be left with an open awareness that catches up everything in and around you in an ecstatic embrace.

4. Don't seek any particular kind of experience; just let yourself be alive in God, however that may be given. You needn't judge your sporadic self-consciousness; you can see such self-consciousness as one functional form of your being, which you don't need to hold on to now. You can trust that you won't lose your real self, only a separating, controlling image of yourself. Your real self is alive in God.

5. Your awareness may be full of feelings or it may be empty; it may be full of thoughts or it may be thoughtless; it may be full of spontaneous praise or it may be calmly open to what is, as it is. If you are in a group, your awareness may spontaneously include others present in all their uniqueness or in all their overlapping, shared spirit, or both. You may spontaneously dance or move with them in some way, or simply move around them. You may be moved to silently bless them with your upraised hands, or simply to appreciate them as they are.

6. As your desire for God lives and you are graced to become freer of inhibitions, you may sense that the different dimensions of your being are coming together in unity. You may be left with a sense of enlivening qualities, such as wholeness, joy, relief, healing, fearlessness, boldness, and love, as though these had been awakened from slumber in you. You may feel the boundaries dropping

between you, others, and God, realizing more fully your mutual belonging.

7. Turn off the music when you are ready. If you are with others, you might form a circle and hold hands in silence, with someone offering some relevant scriptural or other reading, such as Psalm 87:7: "Singers and dancers alike will say, 'All my springs are in you.'"

8. You can be aware that we have joined the ceaseless movement of the cells in our bodies, of the stars, and of everything else in creation, all circling around and within the living heart of God. Then you can sit in silence for another few minutes with a simple, appreciative open presence. After that you can feather out such consciousness into whatever you will be doing after the practice, wanting to bring forward the gist of whatever you've been given in this time that was born of God's Spirit reverberating in your spirit.

If you are in a group for this exercise, you may find yourself feeling much closer to others in the group at the end. You may be vividly aware of the uniqueness of each person and yet feel a shared soul fullness. You may participate more fully in God's love for them, sensing their preciousness in God's eyes. Indeed, you may sense your own eyes seeing others more as God's Spirit in you sees them. You may find yourself wanting to hug them in a way you never before felt free to do or wanting to do. In all this you may taste spiritual community in a heightened way.

Such a sense of presence beyond normal boundaries likely will not last. If it is of God, however, then it will likely leave you with a residue of availability for creative love in your life. Ecstatic awareness, standing outside/beyond our ordinary limited self, may be a foretaste of heaven, but in our broken human situation it's not a fully enduring grace. There seems to be a rhythm of opening and closing of our embodied boundaries that is just a given in human life.

Historically, we find in some churches (and in other traditions as well) a suspicion of such ecstasy. Theologically, this is based primarily on a concern that we might confuse the gift with the Giver. We seek an experience, a high, rather than unconditionally seeking the deepest real: God. The experience can become more of a personal gratification than a true openness to God. We might confuse contrived ecstasy with the real gift of God's Presence in the human heart, which can take many non-ecstatic as well as ecstatic forms.

On a perhaps unconscious psychological level, the suspicion of ecstasy may be based on a fear of losing control and what one might do if that happens. This fear is probably particularly apparent in cultures (and religious subcultures) that cultivate a great deal of emotional reserve and have little active place for the body in its relation to God. On a social-conscience level, there may be the suspicion that religion will become centered on seeking ecstasy and diminish the called-for social fruits of authentic spiritual awareness and commitment.

Every practice has a potential shadow side that obscures its depth of purpose. With proper intent, however, the value of an authentic practice can be embraced, including the value of ecstatically open practices. Theologically, such a practice affirms an embodied spirituality where the body is affirmed as a temple of the Spirit, including bodily senses and movement. Our Spirit-grounded yearnings for our whole being to be caught up in God's Presence, for all the dimensions of our personhood and community to be reconciled with one another in their common Spirit ground, for our full energy to blend into the Spirit-energy and become fully available for loving creative expression—all these deep yearnings are exposed and given scope in such a form of movement prayer as I have described.

As with any authentic practice, we want to enter it with a trust in God and a desire to offer our vulnerable presence in some way. We want to be willing to relinquish anything held separately from the one Love, including any held-over self-images. Then the Spirit moves in our searching, receptive, trusting spirit as it will. A sign of the Spirit's vibrant movement includes some overflow of any sensed loving communion into the broken world's need for that Love. The bold energy stirred in this practice indeed can shape some kind of called-for social fruit, however small or large that may be at a given time.

LITURGICAL MOVEMENT

It's worth noting that movement of the body was often a standard part of the Christian Sunday liturgy in early Christian tradition. The whole congregation participated in processional movements, with different simple rhythmic steps accompanied by chanting, especially of "Alleluia." This practice has been restored and modified in a few contemporary congregations, such as at St. Gregory of Nyssa Episcopal Church in San Francisco. Most Western congregations retain a vestige of this early practice in liturgical processions. In a great many African congregations dancing up the aisle during liturgies is common. Much African American and Pentecostal/Charismatic corporate worship includes what could be called "movement in place," such as swaying to sacred music, raising arms, rhythmic clapping, and moving of the voice in spontaneous praise and pleas.

For many years now across many Christian traditions we have seen sacred movement in the form of liturgical dancers in corporate worship. This form of expression has helped to legitimize again the moving body's place in prayer. The Jewish tradition has its own parallels, as in dancing with the Torah scrolls during the celebration of Simchat Torah. We see other parallels among Hindus, Buddhists, and Native Americans, and in the contemplative Sufi Mevlevi Order. As churches and other religious communities today move toward more focus on spiritual formation and practice involving all dimensions of our humanity, the more likely it will be that bodily movement will find a fuller and deeper sacred place among us.

A FINAL WORD ABOUT MOVEMENT MEDITATION

Probably most of us include some form of the body's movement in our spiritual practice, even if it's simply the sacred gesture of raising our hands or bringing them together for prayer, or moving our bodies forward in church for communion or healing, or some form of meditative walk. Some of us may be called to probe what I have offered here as exercise 5: a simple form of free-form movement meditation as a way of directly disposing our embodied selves to the living Presence.

If you have not included this dimension in your spiritual practice and what I have said draws you to do so, then I hope you will put on some appropriate music soon and open yourself to your larger being in God in whatever way God's Spirit may move you deeper and freer.

CONCLUSION TO THE PRACTICES

These last two more personally involved means of practicing the Presence, icons and movement meditation, share with the previous three practices the potential for a graced open awareness that reveals the same ultimate ground of radiant Love. One way we can prepare to realize this Love more fully is by our willingness to be openly present before our thoughts rise to interpret our experience and before self-images rise, which can limit what is directly known through the innocent spiritual heart.

When we have practiced being present in this way, over time our thoughts and self-images themselves become more transparent to the Presence of God. At that point we understand better why great mystics say that God is in all things and all things are in God.

CHAPTER 3

What Might Be Shown Us
When the Mind Is
in the Heart

First let me share my underlying sense of the omnipresence of grace. Grace, as I understand it, is the gifted involvement of God's Spirit in all dimensions of life. No matter what specifically happens when our spiritual hearts are open, the potential of grace is present. That includes times of seeming nothingness, plainness, dullness, confusion, distraction, heaviness, lightness, fresh awareness, compassion, and everything else that can show up in our consciousness.

Thus, what's important is not the search for some particular experience but bringing to every moment a simple desire to be present to Reality as it is in God, or to put it more personally, present for the divine Beloved through whatever happens. Such a desire carries with it a steady trust that God's Spirit is alive through the full range of the experiences mentioned in the preceding paragraph—alive in ways that may be obscure or manifest to our consciousness.

In that sense it doesn't make much difference what appears during times of openhearted contemplative awareness. You don't have to be disappointed if some of these things never occur. They don't all need to do so. We are present with openness to the Real One, without specific expectations or later judgments. That sincere presence in itself draws our wills into the orbit of grace; even the desire to be present can be seen as a movement of grace.

We will be shown whatever we need to know at a given time (if anything), while grace will work steadily below the surface of our consciousness, where it does most of its healing, awakening, loving work. Our receptivity trusts and welcomes that hidden work. Once in a while some quality of that grace flares to the surface in our contemplative awareness, allowing our consciousness to touch its reality. What's most valuable, though, is our steady, trusting openness to the ongoing hidden work of grace. As John of the Cross made clear, we don't need to understand what's going on in order for God's grace to be effective in us.

The qualities of awareness that I will mention here can be given at any time in our daily lives, not just in set-aside times of meditation or prayer. Some of them can also become more than experiences of the moment. They can expand to become patterns of awareness that are the backdrop for our daily living. Part of the value of set-aside meditation time is the way it helps us embrace our deeper life in God and conditions us to be openly present right through our everyday life. That openness in turn invites God's Spirit to guide our spirits as we are faced with many kinds of discernment during the day.

Even with the best of intentions, most of us easily lose a sense of that open presence as we become caught up in the day's activities, so our separate times of meditation or prayer can become important reminders of the larger Presence in whom we always live and move and have our being. When you see your whole life as an arena for practicing the presence, you will also more likely cultivate blips of practice as you go through the day, such as pausing before you speak and act in order to lean your mind back into your spiritual heart as the seat of where you want your words and actions to come from.

If you are a practitioner of contemplative prayer, then you will likely recognize some of these qualities and could add more.

If you have no experience with contemplative meditation, you may want to skip the rest of this chapter and return to it when you have some experience, which might help you understand more of what I'm trying to convey. The thinking mind on its own has a hard time getting in on what the intuitive mind in the heart shows us.

Love

Our graced moments give us a special perspective on love, which is so central to the divine nature in the Christian-oriented scripture and tradition. God *is* Love, John's Gospel declares, and God is Light. God is thus radiant, enlightened Love, loving Wisdom. Our enlightened knowledge of God in early church descriptions is seen as an experiential knowledge "impregnated with love," as St. Gregory the Great put it.

Radiant Love provides both the seed and cultivation of life. Everything that is, grows from that seed and shares its radiant divine heart, however hidden or warped it may be in creaturely form. Thus, life is made of the divine substance of Love. Eastern Orthodox theology includes a sense of every atom being full of the uncreated energies of God's loving Spirit. The impetus and wisdom for living as one family grow from that Love.

A widow once confided that for several years she had a terrible time moving beyond the grief of her loss. What turned her around was a sudden realization that Love had not died with her husband. She saw that Love indeed *is*—it is latent in everything. She is feeling more in touch now with the Love that lives. This woman knew that Love in a special, precious way with her husband, and yet that particular love was an expression of a larger Love that is always living in different forms in and around us.

In the Christian tradition, God is seen as One, one radiant Love. Yet in the Christian theological tradition, that oneness paradoxically manifests as an interior community of Love, named the Holy Trinity. A contemplatively oriented interpretation of this mystery says that in the trinitarian circle each dimension of the divine Reality, each "role," each "person," flows fully into the others and at the same time receives fully from the others; they are a perfect interdependent unity. We could say that they have no ultimately separate self-image to which they cling, thus freeing them to be inside the whole, yet without loss of distinctiveness as a particular dimension of the divine Wholeness.

When I see myself and all others as made of that one multifaceted Love, I find myself more sensitive to the ways that mutually self-emptying Love shows itself with others in graced moments. Love is given and received simultaneously. Love is circulated, bringing life-giving fruits. It flows in Jesus's way of living and dying, and in the resurrection of the Love that could not be finally buried, because it is the heart of our being, of all being.

Humanity is full of suffering in a broken world so full of denial, distortion, and ignorance of that shared Love ground. But, as St. Paul says, nothing finally can separate us from the love of God that we see in Christ Jesus (Rom 8:38–39). That is the heart of the Christian scripture's good news. It affirms Jesus's declaration that "I have overcome the world" (John 16:33). That "I" is his identification with the Love that is, that was before Abraham, and that will always be. I believe that we all share in that foundational "I" of Love, and when we embrace it as our core identity our lives become oriented to living out who we really are in God, in our own distinctive ways. That basic identity outlasts all the lesser ones and all the brokenness we share in the world, because it grounds us in what is most real and enduring.

This sense of identity was illustrated for me once by a woman who attended a Shalem Institute retreat. She was a member of an ashram, a religious community, in India. She said that when the members passed one another, they would put their hands together, bow, and say, "Om, Thomas," "Om, Mary," or whatever the given name of the person was. "Om" in Sanskrit, in effect, is the largest, most inclusive name for God. It is cognate to the Greek *om* or *on*, "being," found in words like *omnipotent* (all-powerful being) and *omniscient* (all-knowing being). It is sometimes found in Greek on classical icons of Christ, identifying him as an expression of the great imageless "I Am," the "beingness" of God (Exod 3:14).

In such a gesture the members of the religious community recognize one another as sharing the Divine Being, the image of God, while at the same time recognizing the distinctive form of that foundational Love in all its personal particularity. I have often wondered what a difference it would make to the world's well-being if everyone greeted one another in this way! If we belong to a church that includes the ancient exchange of peace in its liturgy, when we take the hand of our neighbor we might keep in mind this wondrous sense of reverence for the person we touch. An old Hasidic story says that a host of angels precedes every person proclaiming: "Make way, make way for the image of God." Indeed!

My trust is that our unique human form, after death to this life, will be transfigured into another form of Love, shaped from the willingness of our little love in this life, within the larger Love's mercy and creativity.

Enabling Confidence

Suspending possessive self-image and willingness to be present in Reality as it is in God, before thoughts arise, can free a steady quality of confidence. Without needing to protect any self-image, and trusting that God is loving Light, I feel able to enter a more openly receptive presence. This quality of confidence is free of any sustained expectations or fears. It invokes instead a willingness just to be available to the mysterious divine Radiance that pervades the whole. Such steady confidence needs to extend through all the endless thoughts and feelings that dart in and out of the mind. I'm tempted to feel frustration and disappointment when I identify these as distractions. However, when I can just accept them as part of what's happening, I can remain trustingly present right through such appearances. I can let thoughts and feelings come and go, intent on steady availability to the Gracious One's Spirit woven through all that is.

Intrinsic Awareness

Through such trusting, willing attentiveness in the space that precedes self-images and thoughts, I have come to know whatever is given in a particular way. When I value this way of immediate intuitive knowing, I can walk through life without having to possess everything with the categories of my mind. I can open the thinking mind's way to this other way of knowing, whereby I come to appreciate people and nature from the inside, from a more direct participation in their being. I often find a sufficiency in this way of knowing. I can just let myself, people, nature, and things unfold together as they do in God's grace with simple appreciation.

Such appreciation from the inside extends to my direct relation to God. When I am graced to be receptively present in love for Love, willing to suspend self-images and thoughts that stand between me and that Love as it is, then for that instant I might find myself closer to the purity of heart that Jesus says enables us to see God (not as an object but as the *subject* in and through whom I see). In such graced, brief moments I become more caught up in Love's living Reality, vulnerable to its movements, humbled by its purifying fire, and astounded by its radiant silence at the heart of what is.

Valuing such intrinsic awareness is different from valuing felt spiritual experience. They are not the same thing. Many great spiritual adepts have downplayed the quest for spiritual experiences because of the latent spiritual materialism in that desire. The desire to possess more spiritual wealth for oneself is a way that paradoxically can keep us separate from realizing our full wealth in God. These spiritual adepts would pray, one way or another, for a reversal of the possessive self's magnetic pull toward accumulation. Instead of focusing on possessing more of God in a way that maintains a central identity with the little self, these adepts would pray that they be empowered to become empty of whatever they clung to of their little self apart from the Real One. Then they would be free to be drawn further into their larger, truer being—their authentic self—in God.

I still find myself valuing spiritual experience and reflection upon it, within the larger frame of trust in the all-encompassing Love that is. The experience can be received in a non-ego-aggrandizing way. It can be received in a way that turns the ego to gratitude and hope for what the experience might do to free us the more for our true being and callings in God.[1]

Such ego-reflective attention to spiritual experience, though, is subordinate to what I have called intrinsic open awareness. Such awareness opens another dimension of contact with deep spiritual reality, different from what our feelings and interpretive mind give us. It involves a stance of aware presence that is attuned to what is, just as it is, before any personal bias affects what we see. It is not screened through any self-image or subjective conditioning. It is pure presence to what is, just as it is.

Awareness of such direct connectedness can leave us more open to grace. However, it also can be captured by a very impure, self-centered self. It's crucial that such a way of knowing from the inside be approached in the context of Love, which is so central in the Christian and other deep spiritual traditions. Without that Love, it can be used to do harm to people and the Earth. Every form of knowledge is subject to misuse. The psychological process involved in inviting an intuitive intrinsic awareness might lead to a capacity for being inside another person's mind at times. That's wonderful if it aids us in knowing and helping them. However, if a person turns this gift to self-centered aims of gaining knowledge to manipulate another person for their own selfish purposes, then it becomes a danger to others.

That probably is one reason that the teaching of deep contemplative awareness historically is hemmed in by other practices and commitments that emphasize loving community. As I earlier reminded us, we live in the reality of a broken human condition, broken off from awareness of the creative Love that shapes us as one family. We suffer all the fear and grasping that emerges from that brokenness. Given that reality, we need a prayerful vigilance that continually looks for centeredness on that Love in ourselves and in others.

On the other hand, if we do approach intrinsic open awareness with a commitment to luminous Love as the heart and purpose of what is, then we can discover a new dimension of loving community: We realize firsthand that everything belongs, that we are distinctive facets of a whole diamond through which shines the same divine Light, however erratically received by our consciousness.

Conclusion

From reading scripture and contemplative saints and listening to others describe their experience as it connects with my own, I believe that one or more of these qualities of open contemplative awareness connects with the deeper and more sustained awareness of many contemplatives through the centuries. Together these qualities point to deep reality as it is immediately, directly known. Our conceptual minds will later stutter to describe, interpret, and connect with the spiritual tradition whatever shows itself in our direct awareness, as I have occasionally done here.

When such touching of reality is inspired by God's Spirit reverberating in our spirits, we are empowered, in the efficacious afterglow of the graced awareness, to be more discerning and free vessels of the creative Love that has moved us.

Because that Love, that heart of Reality, is integrally woven through our future, it cannot be finally defeated by the other God-permitted separating forces in and around us that challenge it. I know how often I succumb to those forces, but each such succumbing, for all its pain and confusion, can be a *felix culpa*, a happy fault, through which I am drawn the more to the one enduring real Force, the loving, merciful energy of God out of which our being, awareness, and freedom are shaped.

PART II

Vital Contemplative Gifts for Our Spiritual Communities and Global Family

Contemplative Gifts for Congregations and Other Intentional Spiritual Communities

The Promise of Contemplative Groups

Amazing things can happen to people when they are part of a group of spiritually seeking and ready people who are willing to gather together for contemplative prayer over time. I have come to believe that intensively structured spiritual communities are little tastes of heaven from which most of us can benefit in our lives, whatever different form these groups may take related to people's situations, religious background, and callings. The community may have an ongoing life together in other ways (as in a congregation), but coming together for unambiguous receptive presence in God for a protected period of time is a vital dimension of its life, one that can positively affect all the other dimensions of an ongoing group's life.

We see the cultivation of this and other forms of intensive spiritual community in all religious traditions. Jesus going off with his disciples to pray in solitude, and then bringing the fruits of that time to their collective life and mission, is a prime example. Other examples are found in monastic communities, in the retreats taken in monasteries over the years by millions of people who have come to temporarily participate in that way of life, in spiritual centers, in spiritual direction, and in what we see happening today in many congregations.

Whatever its form, an authentic contemplatively oriented retreat or ongoing group is carefully structured to bring attention to our wider identity and purpose in God. It will include enough silence to give vivid room for the divine Mystery to show its delicate, subtle Presence: as beauty, love, purifier, wisdom giver, inspirer of what is called for, or in whatever other ways that radiant loving Presence may show itself.

Bringing Group Experience into Daily Living

The heavenly moments found in such a shared open spiritual community, whatever the community's form, can vanish pretty quickly in the face of our human brokenness, even if there is some residue of greater sensitivity and compassion. It's amazing how quickly we can fall into a protective, assertive ego level of self-identity and relationship in a way that can eclipse the delicate open awareness we had only a few moments ago. Practicing the presence in dedicated separate periods of time is one thing; doing it through all the ordinary activities and relationships of our day can be quite another.

The set-aside times can help condition us to at least minimally remember who we are on a deeper level in those ordinary times. We can complement those set-aside times with dedicated special practices that help us remember life happening within the orbit of grace as we move through the events of the day. However, for most of us it's not easy to maintain our sane spiritual identity when it is no longer being invited by the people and situations around us.

Heaven and its shalom are not likely to be an experienced reality much of the time, but when we have at least tasted its possibility in brief times of spiritual community and graced meditation, that taste lingers in our lives. It reminds us that there is more to life than the grasping and fearing we know on the ego level. We then can be a little more playful on the ego level, because we don't tightly identify with it for so long a time. We more easily let it be a functional surface self, a vessel of our larger being in God, and not the definer of who we ultimately are. Even when ego-identity has kidnapped us, little Spirit-glimmers will likely show up in time to remind us that we and our neighbor are more than our culture and our little ego-self would say that we are.

However sporadically, we then can find ourselves empowered to bring a dimension of spiritual heart awareness to situations, a dimension that is more in touch with Reality as it is in God. We are freer to be in the unique moment, available to the living Beloved's fragrance in and beyond us, through whatever is happening. Then, both individually and collectively, we may find ourselves able to let situations unfold and show us larger possibilities of understanding and action, guided by whatever form of creative love is being invited.

Contemplative Orientation in Different Forms of Spiritual Community

Where is such intensive contemplative awareness being cultivated today, beyond centers like the Shalem Institute? Today we may have more places where we can turn than have ever been available historically. However, as with every human endeavor, we need to be discerning in where we go. A particular spiritual center may be authentic, but what it offers is just not right for us. In our often normless, anything goes spiritual atmosphere, what is offered also may be too narrow, shallow, cultic, disrespectful of the different ways Spirit moves people, ungrounded in the deep spiritual/contemplative tradition, or otherwise inauthentic for us. Let me single out just a few particular contexts of contemplative community for special attention.

SPIRITUAL DIRECTION

The smallest spiritual community is two people together, in the form of informal spiritual friendship or of a more committed ongoing formal relationship together, usually going by such names as spiritual companionship, friendship, or spiritual direction. One value of having an experienced spiritual companion is to help us sift through the possibilities of community in relation to our own particular situation and calling. An ongoing relationship with such a spiritual companion (or with a small group of companions), usually meeting monthly, also gives us an accountable place where we can attend the mysterious movements of God's Spirit in our lives and our responses to them. For Christians, such a relationship connects with Jesus's declaration that "where two or three are gathered in my name, there I am among them" (Matt 18:20).

Spiritual direction has been growing by leaps and bounds in recent decades.[1] That is no accident, given (1) a cultural environment that increasingly puts the weight of spiritual discernment on the individual rather than on any religious or other communal body, and (2) the growing sense of the spiritual journey as a lifetime affair of listening and responding to the Spirit. It can be a great gift to have someone with us listening and probing for the deepest, truest voice amid the cacophony of sounds.

The greatest gift of a contemplative orientation to such a spiritual companionship is the way it can encourage us to embrace our desire to live from our deep being in God in the moment. This hope is cultivated by leaning back together into an open awareness between our thoughts, available for what is given in that receptive place of the spiritual heart. In this process, we are sitting heart to heart with each other, beneath the personality and the contitional mind levels of presence. I have said much more about this in several previous books on spiritual direction.

MONASTIC COMMUNITIES AND THEIR ASSOCIATES

Monastic communities are the oldest continuous form of intensive spiritual community in Western Christianity. They bring forward a stable and mature form of the early experiments with community among the desert mothers and fathers. The primary aim of deepening conversion of life in God through a vowed lifetime—the daily rhythm of corporate and personal prayer, labor, study, and recreation together, and a rhythm of corporate silence and speaking—with a group of others who are likewise committed has been an anchor in the storms of Western Christian history since the sixth century. Many other forms of monastic and apostolic (i.e., those having a mission focus in the world that draws them outside steady residential common life) communities have emerged since then, with varying rhythms of shared life together.

A great many of these communities are in decline in Western countries today in terms of membership: people willing to commit themselves permanently to the primary monastic vows of poverty, chastity, and obedience. However, many of them are very much alive as places where lay and ordained people flock for short-term retreats. They are havens of quiet, prayer, and a spacious, sane rhythm of life that can help free people to recognize their deeper selves in God.

Beyond being places of retreat, for some people they become places that form part of their identity. Retreatants may eventually become oblates or associates of the community in some form, taking up a personal rule of life inspired by their experience in the community and assisted by the monastery's members and tradition. The rule usually consists of certain spiritual practices adapted to the particular person's situation, practices that have the effect of feathering out a sense of a monastic-inspired larger personal and communal identity and purpose into ordinary daily life. Such a rule of life also has been taken up today by a number of people completely apart from any experience or relationship with a monastic community.[2]

Monastic communities most often are Roman Catholic (a few are Anglican or Eastern Orthodox), but many of them have welcomed a growing number of Protestants and others who have asked to become associated. The contemplative grounding of monastic communities, together with a commitment to hospitality, has frequently led to their openness to people regardless of denominational background at the level of guests and associates (although not in terms of membership, except in rare cases, such as the ecumenical Taize community in France).

In Celtic (as well as Anglo-Saxon) Christianity in the British Isles between the fifth and eleventh centuries (i.e., until the Norman Conquest), the monastery, rather than the parish church, was the normal center of spiritual life for the people. At the heart of such a community was a dedicated core of monks who followed a strict rule of life and provided worship, counseling, education, the arts, and hospitality for all kinds of people. They were accompanied by married and single people with a less strict rule of life who lived within or near the monastic grounds. What we know of this inclusive model of spiritual community can stimulate our imagination about how to best understand and form spiritual community in our time, as a number of modern writers and spiritual leaders have pointed out.[3]

OTHER SPIRITUAL CENTERS

In the last few decades we have seen a growing number of contemplatively oriented spiritual centers and groups forming, often on the grounds of apostolic religious communities that have experienced a decline in membership and have discerned a call to turn over more of their space for retreats and workshops related to the spiritual life. In the United States and Canada alone, there are hundreds of retreat centers that provide space for guided and unguided individual and group silent retreats, sometimes with the availability of a spiritual director.

Many of them also offer a variety of spiritually oriented workshops and ongoing groups. Some of them offer contemplative practices from other deep faith traditions beyond the Christian. Several have been bases for the beginning of worldwide movements for particular forms of contemplative prayer and understanding, which I will mention soon. Most of them have Roman Catholic or Anglican roots, but a growing number of Protestant centers are emerging. For example, the Upper Room's Academy for Spiritual Formation sponsors two-year and shorter-term spiritual formation programs and offers residencies around the country. The Renovaré movement is another such sponsor of programs, grounded more in the Evangelical tradition. The ecumenical Shalem Institute focuses especially on long-term extension programs for contemplative life and leadership.

I have found many of these centers to be harbingers of a more open and focused future for spiritual community: places that offer intensive opportunities for deeper spiritual understanding, support, and practice for anyone who is ready, and sometimes places where a socially prophetic sense of the church's life and mission is fostered.

In my own experience, most of the specialized spiritual centers are very welcoming of all who come, regardless of denomination or any religious affiliation at all. When it comes to the deeper spiritual life, there is a natural ecumenism that transcends many historical faith differences. The Holy Spirit has a way of suspending the boundaries that we set up. As Rumi once put it, "Love's creed is separate from all religions: The creed and denomination of lovers is God."[4]

These spiritual centers provide inspiring oases of inclusive spiritual community and often of contemplatively oriented practices for thousands of people. Two monastic centers have spawned international organizations. One, Contemplative Outreach, grew out of the practice of Centering Prayer, led by one of the original proponents of that contemplative prayer form, the Cistercian Thomas Keating. The other, The World Community for Christian Meditation, was founded by the Benedictine John Main and carried on after his death by another Benedictine, Laurence Freeman. This body focuses on a bit different method of contemplative prayer that some would see as more mantra-like than Centering Prayer. Both movements are grounded in small ecumenical contemplative prayer groups meeting around the world.

In a recent joint letter from both leaders, they state a common contemplative heritage, with special respect for the early monastic tradition and the medieval mystics, and a shared larger purpose of encouraging contemplative awareness that contributes to the renewal of the churches, an enhanced sense of the sacred in the modern world, and courage for peacemaking, social justice, and interreligious dialogue.

All these spiritual centers form a vital complement to the rest of the church's life today. Those participants who are clergy and laypeople in parishes often take back to their congregations something of the inspiration they have found in those centers, which can serve the imagination and deepening of the congregation's life.

Now let me turn to the local church's place as a potential center of contemplative orientation that can move people toward a more profound way of touching their own and others' deep reality and calling in God.

THE SPIRITUAL COMMUNITY OF THE LOCAL CHURCH

During the fourth to sixth centuries, after Christianity was accepted into the mainstream of life in the Roman Empire, thousands of people sought a more fervent spiritual life and community in the deserts of North Africa and the Near East. Some lived alone as hermits; some formed loose, mutually supportive communities; and others later formed more structured community life. All of them valued silence, in which they opened themselves to God through scripture, prayer, and manual labor. Some of the more saintly and available of these desert fathers and mothers were sought out by thousands of Christians from across the Roman Empire, people who were seeking advice and spiritual nurture from them.

Over the centuries these desert communities grew into many different forms of monastic community with a variety of emphases in practice and mission. By the late Middle Ages, people, especially in Europe, had a great variety of spiritual communities available to them, including the parish church; monasteries; apostolic, mission-oriented religious communities (such as the Franciscans and Dominicans); and different forms of lay guilds and associations. In the Reformation, monastic and other religious communities were rejected by the Protestant Reformers, and the local church, along with the family, became the locus of spiritual community for Protestants. In the Counter Reformation, the Roman Catholic parish church also was given more emphasis, at least in part to centralize church authority there in the face of the splintering of the church in the Reformation.

THE CONTEMPORARY CONGREGATION

Increasingly, local churches are becoming the base for much new spiritual exploration. This is symbolized in the way the term *spiritual formation* has come to be seen as a significant dimension of Christian education in many congregations. Such a term assumes that there is a lifetime process of spiritual maturation and not just a childhood of religious learning and an adulthood of spiritual stasis. Life increasingly is seen as an evolving individual and communal spiritual journey, full of the Spirit's surprises, callings, and growing freedom for life in Love.

This new concern for deeper spiritual understanding, practice, and Spirit-led transformation throughout one's life cuts across all denominational and liberal and conservative boundaries. In this phenomenon, God's Spirit is enlarging the boundaries, traditions, and practices of a great many churches. Thus, this emerging situation of spiritual hunger and openness in congregations is not only providing an opportunity for further personal and congregational spiritual awakening but also drawing people together across old, hard historical religious boundaries.

The pattern of the paschal mystery in the spiritual life is applicable here, worded in this case in terms of dying to whatever Spirit no longer inhabits in a life-giving way and rising to join whatever the Spirit is birthing that spirals us further into the realization of our true life and community in God.

To the extent this new openness reflects the larger work of the Spirit in the spiritual hunger we see beyond the church in the culture as a whole, it also has an evangelical dimension. Many religiously unaffiliated people are spiritually searching. If they can sense that what a church offers in response is, not a straightjacket that narrows their quest for the authentic largeness and mystery of the Holy (a fear that I believe underlies many people's exclamation that "I'm spiritual, but not religious"), but a lifejacket that gives them a way to authentic and sustained life and community in God, then such people can find a home for their souls in the local church.

I believe a new church is slowly emerging as this fresh attention to life in the Spirit becomes front and center in a congregation's life. It is new in combining openness to the mysterious largeness and intimacy of divine Graciousness, a wide spectrum of spiritual practices, appreciation of many mature spiritual adepts in history, the dynamism of life in the living Spirit, and the intrinsic connection of spiritual life with spiritual community and social concern. At the same time such an emerging church is old

in its continuity with these same qualities found in different com-
binations historically in mature spiritual communities.

This emergence is influenced by the fragmented social
context in which so many people live today. As Diana Butler
Bass says:

> Many if not most contemporary people live as vagrants
> —spiritually, intellectually, geographically, morally, and
> relationally. Vague awareness of this new reality creates
> much social anxiety and can potentially fuel funda-
> mentalisms, inquisitions, and culture wars....In an age
> of fragmentation, it may well be the case that the voca-
> tion of congregations is to turn [vagrant] tourists into
> pilgrims—those who no longer journey aimlessly, but,
> rather, those who journey in God and whose lives are
> mapped by the grace of Christian practices....[The
> congregation can become] a kind of open monastic
> community—a place of spiritual practices, hospitality,
> worship, and justice...an intentional way of life.[5]

Bass's term *open monastic community* recalls what I said earlier
in this chapter about the Celtic Christian precedent of the
monastery as the disciplined center of an interactive larger community of committed laypeople, who share in the hospitality and
educational, artistic, and worship life of the monastic community.
Those havens of spiritual community often existed in times similar
to our own in terms of social disruption, change, and violence in
the larger society.

One of the most important things we can learn from the
Celtic experience for the modern congregation is the significance of
a group of spiritually disciplined, committed people at the core of
the community, people whose personal and communal identities
and actions are grounded in openness to God as liberating and loving light. This core group sees the community primarily as an

organism mysteriously growing from God's grace, rather than as an organization that they can effectively construct from autonomous rational decisions. Cultivation of such a sense of community in God, led by a core group of committed leaders, is a thread that can be pulled through the whole life of the congregation.[6]

The flowering of such a community in a way that involves every dimension of its life will likely involve a considerable period of time, as will become clear below.

Contemplative Contributions

Contemplative practices and their underlying understanding and trust of Spirit-presence can offer a deepening of individual—and often of congregational—spiritual openness and way of life over time. I have seen or heard of this evolution in a variety of churches over the past thirty-five years.

Although the Spirit is free to create transforming firestorms, as at Pentecost, my experience is that over the long haul we're talking about the slow, jagged, sporadic awakening of people to their deeper nature in God and its gradual overflow into a different way of being and acting in church, as well as in the rest of their lives. The spiritual journey has no end point in this life. It is an ongoing revelation of transforming intuitions of the holy Presence. We come to see ourselves involved in an ongoing seasoning through the sea of divine intimacy that pervades life moment by moment.

Unlike a specialized spiritual center, a congregation carries a vast range of purposes and functions for people. As in a family, each member must bear (and, hopefully, sometimes celebrate) the very different spiritual and personal places that each of them inhabit.

That is one reason why shared worship is so vital to congregational life. Like a Spirit-grounded family Thanksgiving meal, it becomes an event that can transcend the differences and draw people together. In the liturgy they can share, in their own different ways, a sense of the availability of divine Love and their collective participation in that Love. (I will say more about the liturgy soon.)

Contemplative awareness needs to begin on the personal level. Through contemplative practices we need time to realize what such disposition to Reality in God can do to give the Spirit room to shed layers of illusion and willfulness in us, to reveal the Love at the core of our being, and to free spontaneous compassion and a more discerning mind. We need time to really set our desire firmly on the realization of true life in the Love that births us. We need to embrace the ongoing conversion of life that gives us eyes to see everything happening within the orbit of divine grace.

Church assistance for this kind of personal awareness through such avenues as contemplative prayer groups, retreats, workshops, guided silence in liturgies, and spiritual direction helps to establish a beachhead in the congregation for a contemplative orientation. The fresh eyes and hearts that people can be given on that beachhead in time lifts their heads beyond the beach to the larger horizon of their lives, including the congregation's life.

Spiritual awakening is never for us alone. The Spirit shows itself to be a very public as well as personal face of God. What happens to us, like an energized wave drawn to the shore, is meant to refresh and reshape the shore as needed. We bring what's been given to us into the situations of our lives—in this case, the congregation—and what's been given to us interacts with what's been given to others. That interaction, pervaded by the Spirit's presence, leavens decisions in meetings, the expression of our liturgies and homilies, education, mission projects, and the rest of the life of the church.

Of course, this becomes much truer when we are meeting with others who also are open to the movements of Spirit among us. We all know that is not always the case. Like every other institution, the church is made up of flawed, fearful, partly closed, distracted people, and none of us is immune to our own version of such brokenness. We expect more of the church though, and we are more easily moved to despair and alienation when we don't find much difference there. A contemplative consciousness helps in so far as it can leave us a little more playful on the ego level, a little lighter and more patient, biding the Spirit's timing for things. At the same time it can also leave us freer to act when the moment for action arrives. Contemplative consciousness also can bring a little more spiritual confidence, drawing us to trust the intimate Love that sustains our freedom to be flawed, shows us to be precious and blessed images of God, and opens the way to larger life.

Despite and through the messy mix of people who companion one another in the congregation, the Spirit is beckoning contemplative consciousness further into congregational life today. We can move beyond the sideshow where contemplative formation has been restricted to a small group of people praying together, even as that may be a valuable beginning point in a congregation's life. That sideshow has been around in a number of churches for many years now, and it is beginning in many more. As the Spirit readies us, we need to move beyond this marginalization to the main stage, looking at the potential fruit of a contemplative orientation at the heart of a congregation's purpose and activities.

Let me now introduce a larger framework of faith formation as a valuable context for bringing a contemplative orientation to bear in the congregation's life more generally.

Faith and a Contemplative Orientation

In 2001 the Shalem Institute began a special extension program for the contemplative spiritual deepening and leadership of congregationally based clergy. One of the staff members of that program, Robert Duggan, a nationally respected pastor and an author concerning parish life, helped us to look at what he called faith or spiritual formation in nine key areas of congregational common life, which I will spell out shortly.

Over time, the reinforcement of a faith orientation through every dimension of the congregation's life helps to evolve a congregational subculture that is increasingly aware of its difference from some of the values of the dominant culture. It becomes far more than a mirror of the larger culture with a marginal religious overlay. People come to support one another in exploring and embracing a coherent faith orientation in all areas of life. This orientation becomes the central ground for relationships and decision making together.

Agreeing on a common faith orientation is not easy, however, given its very nature. A faith orientation is broader than a contemplative orientation. It is the larger common and personal ground that we have received from our tradition's basic religious teaching and practice, drawn from scripture, theology, liturgy, and history. This teaching and practice interacts with our unique personal experience. The outcome of that interaction is a personally distinctive adaptation of the faith and its implications for personal and communal life, which overlaps in varying degrees with that of others in the congregation. As people's experience and reflection evolve over time, their understanding of faith and its implications will likely evolve as well.

Thus, every congregation has a broadly shared set of moral and spiritual practices and religious history, but the members form a spectrum of different interpretations and emphases. For the sake of unity, members of every congregation try to embrace common ground wherever possible and either gingerly ignore or respectfully debate their differences. However, when the differences are strongly held, they can become more important than unity and lead the congregation into serious conflict. At its best, the conflict will lead to deeper prayer and a willingness to let the

Spirit draw the congregation toward common spiritual ground that is deeper than the conflict.

Much faith orientation is developed on the level of the thinking and feeling mind. A contemplative orientation brings to prominence the way we see life from the spiritual heart. From that place of more intuitive, receptive immediacy, we become aware of an overarching inclusiveness of life in God. We realize that with all our differences we flow from the same Holy One, who can never be fully grasped by our minds. Our life, work, and prayer finally belong within the same family of grace as everyone else's. Our salvation, our wholeness in God, is not a private affair; it is part of a shared larger movement of grace. As attention to the spiritual heart is threaded through the whole faith-formation process, it can contribute to a deeper sense of mutual belonging and keep the conflicts that rise in larger perspective.[7]

On the congregational level, this affirms the value of bearing both the pain and joy of continuing to seek shared life and reconciliation with people very different from ourselves, because, finally, they are our mirrors and we are theirs. Sometimes, of course, the dominant and tightly held values of a particular congregation leave us with too little breathing room for our souls and spiritual values. Then we may need to seek out a different congregation or other spiritual community where we feel sufficient overlap in faith understanding and acceptance to sustain a life-giving communal relationship and to give room for contemplative grounding to deepen.

Let me turn now to Robert Duggan's nine essential dimensions of parish/congregational life, each of which is important to faith formation. A full formation process needs to involve the contemplative spiritual heart as well as our thinking and feeling minds.[8]

  1. *Communal Ritual*: liturgy and other sacramental, healing, and worship occasions.

2. *The Word*: proclaimed, reflected upon, interpreted, and applied.
3. *Formal Catechesis* (education): aimed at transformation rather than just information.
4. *Service Experiences*: where we live into new ways of being and understanding, including reflection on service experiences from a faith perspective.
5. *Skills Training*: for grounding life deeply in God, such as prayer and discernment.
6. *New Member Processes*: focused on intentional faith and committed belonging.
7. *Opportunities for Social Interaction*: affective bonding with people of faith, seeing the world through their eyes.
8. *Public Witness of Members*: multiplying opportunities for sharing one's faith journey.
9. *Leadership Structures/Functioning*: communicating spiritual values by the way we function (lead and work) together.

If you are involved in a congregation, I invite you—alone or, even better, with others—to reflect on each of these areas in the light of your sense of what's important in faith formation grounded in contemplative awareness. Between us, we can bring forward a fuller sense of possibilities that can encourage and stimulate one another.

I am not able to address all nine of these areas here in terms of contemplative grounding, but I would like to offer a few examples of what can be done in one of these areas, communal ritual. If you are involved in a congregation, what I say, hopefully, will give you some stimulus for your own reflection on this and the other eight dimensions. In chapter 7 I mention a few contemplatively oriented resources related to the third area mentioned by Robert Duggan: spiritual formation of both adults and children.

Two necessary conditions need to be mentioned for the examples I give—and indeed for the extension of contemplative awareness to any area of the congregation's life. First, someone needs to be significantly involved who has enough firsthand experience with contemplative open awareness to be able to discerningly bring it to bear in the way they see and respond to what is happening in any particular area. That person needs to have a sense that a contemplative orientation can lead to undreamed of Spirit-guided possibilities in the life and mission of the congregation over time. There may be more than one such leader available, but at least one is vital.

Second, most of the other people working with that leader in the development of a particular dimension of the congregation's life need to be open to a contemplative orientation, even if they have no formal experience with it themselves. Informally, many people, without naming it "contemplative," can recognize at least something of what contemplative awareness is from their own experience. It isn't some esoteric capacity; it's a dimension of availability to reality as it is in the moment, in God. This capacity belongs to everyone, however unconscious and undeveloped it may be. Each of us is a capacity for God, although fully realized communion/union with God is not in our hands: that is sheer gift.

Liturgy

Coming together for formal weekly worship is the central shared act found in all Christian traditions. Why is this so consistently true historically and today? The answers are manifold, but let me posit just one here: our psyches are put together in such a way that if we don't come together within a week, we are more likely to forget who we most truly are in God—personally and communally. This is especially true for the average person who is faced with competing views of reality in daily life and who does not have any other spiritual community or significant daily spiritual practice that reinforces a deeper identity. Such people really need to strive at least for a daily prayer practice of some kind, though, to embody their desire for deeper life in God. Without it, unreal expectations are placed on what the weekly gathering can offer.

The weekly Christian liturgy is a time of memory, reconnecting our personal story with the tradition's holy stories of divine-human interaction, with special attention to Jesus's story. It's also a time of hope, as the stories, homilies, prayers, and calls for action open the possibility of a just, reconciled, and loving future oriented toward God. Further, it's a time of caringly connecting with others who share this larger sense of identity and purpose.

A layperson once told me that the liturgy is the only time in his week where he relates to a body of people in a nonutilitarian way. In this gathering for worship, everyone is just who they are; he relates to them as end-in-themselves valued fellow human beings, who together celebrate belonging to a larger, loving, guiding divine Reality within which they all have intrinsic worth.

All of this speaks to the larger shared faith dimension of the gathering. We're turned from the temptations of a narrower sense of ego-self during the week toward a larger sense of identity in relation to God and other people.

What does contemplative open awareness bring to such a time? Above all, it can undergird memory, hope, and communal gathering with a sense of the living Presence being right here, now, before as well as in our thoughts and feelings. As we are seeing, hearing, and doing in that time from within our open spiritual heart (however erratically), we are encountering everything as it is in the inclusive living Presence. Everything, everyone—past, present, and future—have their place in the eternal gracious Presence, which is in our midst.

An Eastern Orthodox view of the Sunday liturgy points to this sense of living Presence when it speaks of entering the church (whose very architecture is designed to represent the whole cosmos) and the divine liturgy (which is mystically sung, expressing a great saving mystery beyond the mind's analytical grasp) as entering heaven.

If heaven is living in the eternal gracious divine Presence with the whole company of heaven, then our time in church is one of foreshadowing this Reality on Earth, living into it as we are able, recognizing the mysterious larger Love available in all that is happening, and yearning for its full realization everywhere on Earth (indeed in all creation) as it is in heaven. In the purest moments life is seen together through God's eyes in our intuitive spiritual hearts. Such transforming awareness can shape what we then think, feel, and do.

Few of my readers are likely Eastern Orthodox, and few of us are graced to know many such pure moments, but there are things we can do that give room for this larger view of presence in our own liturgies. Given the many conflicting concerns of the people who gather, the liturgy needs to be as powerful an invitation to God-openness as it was for that Russian delegation in the tenth century who attended a Byzantine liturgy in search of a church to recommend to their sovereign for the Russian people. They left converted, feeling the mystical power carried by the liturgy so movingly that they felt they had been in heaven.

One issue that people bring relates to our ambivalence about trusting our deep being in God enough to be open to the transforming changes that might come from letting ourselves be vulnerable to Christ's Spirit during the liturgy. We yearn for such deepening conversion, and at the same time we fear what we might lose. We want to be in communion with God, but in such a way that we keep all we have. Our confused, protective egos would prefer an add-on to what we know and have, not a transfiguration that reorients our lives.

I can remember attending a Sunday Eucharist once that seemed to illustrate the triumph of the fearful side of that ambivalence. The liturgy was like an efficient express train leaving a station on time and bound to arrive at the next station at the predetermined time. It was so speedily efficient and mechanical, so spaceless for the Spirit, that I was left feeling as though it was an unconscious desperate attempt to evade God in the name of God. We will do what we have to do here to tip our hat to our larger Being, but we will do it in a way that we can get through it without allowing that Being vulnerable room where we can be opened to its transforming Presence. The Spirit seemed to be left imprisoned and fossilized in the overcontrolled words, acts, and speed of the liturgy.

The leaders who guarded the gate of entry weren't free to unlock the prison door and invite the Spirit to open hearts and minds to their deep divine ground. It seemed a lost opportunity, but the Spirit never gives up her availability in Christ. I'm sure she burst the bonds of such a prison and found her way into at least some hearts, in however subdued a manner. And then there would be next week. Maybe the trust would be greater than the fear then. The Spirit would have more room to breathe her life into people.

Contemplative Possibilities in Corporate Worship

Here are a few suggestions that can help open the way for people's firsthand presence in the Presence during a Sunday liturgy or other time of corporate worship.

Above all, give room for silence. John of the Cross said that silence is God's first language. Mother Teresa (who required of her sisters two hours of silent daily prayer) said that silence is God speaking to us. Isaac of Nineveh advocated loving silence above all things, because "it brings you near the fruit which the tongue is too weak to interpret....If you love truth, then you must love silence...for silence will even unite you with God."[9]

Meister Eckhart said that there is nothing so like God as silence. Silence, then, isn't just a means. In its fullness, silence itself is participation in God's Being, which is the depth of our own being. Such intimate participation is available to everyone, across every linguistic and cultural divide, since silence is a language that everyone knows.

Silence thus is living, pregnant, sacred space, open presence before sounds emerge and from which sounds (including thoughts) emerge. Silence is boundaryless, inclusive of everything, full of possibilities. It is spaciousness that can draw us deeper into Reality as it is, deeper into the delicate gracious Presence that inhabits the silence, leaving us more available to the Holy One's healing, transforming, enlightening grace.

Silence approached with this understanding leads to seeing the importance of a rhythm between silence and sound in liturgy. If we have silence when we enter, we have space to lean back into the larger Presence pervading the church. In that leaning back we have a means of letting go the surface-jangling thoughts that easily kidnap us. If we have brief attentive silence before and longer silence after scriptural readings and the homily, we have space to hear more deeply and absorb what's meant for us. A period of open congregational prayer beginning in silence could lead the prayers to rise from God's deep prayer in us. If the sacramental meal is part our liturgy, that can be received and followed with a vulnerable, silent heart, inviting room for the awesome Presence to be itself, living in us however it lovingly will. (I will return to the subject of Eucharist soon.)

In my experience, the homily sometimes can involve guided silence. For example, if the Gospel lesson is a story about Jesus, after it has been read the congregation could be invited to join the scene of that story; then they can be left alone with Jesus for a while. People can just let themselves be openly present in his presence, available for silent communion or for whatever question or expression to him may spontaneously rise within or for whatever word or act of his living Spirit that may be given.

Such an opportunity allows people to let their minds sink to their spiritual hearts, where they can be directly in the living Presence in a very concrete way. I especially remember an older priest in a congregation who joyfully confided in me after the service that while he was being guided into silence with Jesus by the story in the Gospel lesson (the story of Bartimaeus), he had directly experienced Christ's gracious living presence for the first time in his life. Certainly the imagination may be at work during such times, but when the door of the heart is open, so is the deeper voice of the One who lovingly knows us and through whom we know.

There may be other places in the liturgy where you find that silence could invite fuller direct awareness of divine Presence. The period following Communion is a good example. The Benedictine Laurence Freeman observes that the mystical dimension of the Eucharist is that in its silent heart we taste and enter the silence of God, from whom the Word eternally springs: silence in the Eucharist "refreshes language, [it] restores...meaning especially to oft-quoted, familiar texts. Without silence even sacred words can become noise, babble....St. Ignatius of Antioch said that if we cannot understand the silence of Christ we will not be able to understand his words either. We can only understand his silence by being silent ourselves." Freeman goes on to say:

> Silence in the Eucharist does not threaten emptiness or denote absence but exposes presence and invites responsiveness....It draws the community closer together and unifies their attention so that together in mind and heart they can hear the word and share in the mystery....At the conclusion [of such a Eucharist

in his experience], there is a sense of thankfulness and refreshment, not relief that we were finished....Unless we have come together at a deep level in its celebration the closing words "Go in peace" will mean we go in pieces, just as we probably arrived. Silence allows the full meaning of the Eucharist at its deepest, post-verbal levels of sacramental efficacy to unfold in our lives.[10]

Such an emphasis on silence in the Eucharist is doubly needed and appreciated in the context of the flood of noise and often trivial and commercially oriented voices in our culture, which can drown out people's sense of a larger Presence and Voice. People's deep souls are starved for meaningful space that allows them room to see and feel life from the openness of their spiritual hearts rather than the drivenness of their overstuffed minds, an openness where they can touch their own and life's wholeness in God.

If you begin to include more such silence in communal worship, it's important to prepare the congregation for that if it is new to them, including the preparation of children, reinforced in church school classes (which the type of children's church school materials I mention in chapter 7 do well). In our culture we are so geared to see silence as worthless or fearful that people have a conditioned tendency to either just become numb during that time or else to let it be filled with many restless, random thoughts.

The unprogrammed meeting branch of the Religious Society of Friends (Quakers) makes the silence itself the primary container for the entire service. People speak spontaneously out of the living silence as they may be moved by the Spirit to share a message for the others present. Even when no one speaks, however, there is a shared sense that the act of gathering together in silence, available to God with and for one another, carries the heart of corporate worship.

Besides silence, another contemplative element related to corporate worship that I would hold up is silence's seeming opposite: sound. The mind wants to be in on what's happening through whatever words can offer in terms of story, understanding, and inspiration through the liturgy and homily. The words can be heard with the mind in the heart, listening (and, where called for, speaking) from the place from which deep words come.

Music, instrumental and sung, can draw the mind to the heart at various levels. It can help to open a felt presence and a sense of inclusive belonging: everyone here is part of me and I of them, and together we are part of the larger gracious Reality we call God. Sometimes such presence is opened through music to the point of ecstasy, where one's whole being is brought together in one transcendent expression of praise and wide-open awareness.

Silence and sound are intimately related. When sounds come, if we sense them as particular shapings of the ever-pregnant silence rather than as something qualitatively different, then we can absorb sounds while still being grounded in the spacious silence. The silence need not disappear when sounds come. If they are made of the silence, particular shapings of the silence, then they still carry the sacred spaciousness from which they come.

Open awareness is grounded in the vast intimacy of silence, and it can continue right through all the sounds we hear if they are seen as shapings of the infinite potential of silence rather than distractions from it. My own experience tells me how difficult it is to maintain such open awareness evenly through sound and silence, and yet ever since I was taught such contemplative intimacy of sound and silence long ago, it has opened up at least the possibility of living with sounds in a way that they do not as often take me away from the spaciousness of the silence, and the One who communes, whispers, and sings through the silence.[11]

Conclusion

In this chapter I have touched on a few key dimensions of intentional spiritual community in the light of a contemplative understanding, enough hopefully for you to note the difference that contemplative open awareness can make. I hope it has helped to stimulate your own sense of what is important and possible in your life of spiritual community at various levels. In chapter 7 I will look more carefully at some ways such spiritual community can be further fostered and deepened through spiritual formation in a variety of educational settings.

In the next chapter I will expand the sense of community beyond our intentional spiritual gatherings to our ways of being present in the larger life of the world. I will probe some key contributions that a contemplative orientation can make to the global village we share.

CHAPTER 5

Gifts for the Larger World

How does the world appear when we are seeing with our mind in our heart, with contemplative open awareness? Not long ago, I was graced to be present in this way for a brief period during one of my daily prayer/meditation times. I had just begun to pray the Lord's Prayer. I was suddenly overwhelmed with the first word, *Our*. I couldn't go any further. That word revealed to me the fullness of community to which I belonged. Nothing was outside "Our"; everything formed and happening, all time—past, present, and future—was interconnected. I realized that all that is, intrinsically is part of my community, and vice versa: all I am, intrinsically is part of the larger inclusive community.

As Thich Nhat Hanh has put it, we live in "inter-being." Neuroscientists point to a part of our brain that is geared to compassion, to recognizing our caring connectedness to other beings. James Fowler points to the "universalizing" dimension of faith development, where we recognize such connectedness in the most inclusive way.

The awareness of our mutual belonging puts in perspective our more exclusive belongings that can fragment us and the world. The most exclusive sense of belonging is to our self alone. Such a sense, on its positive side, allows us to bring our unique, called-out resources into the larger community. When that exclusive self-identity shows its dark side, however, we succumb to one or more of the classical list of deadly sins: arrogant pride, covetousness, lust, envy, gluttony, anger, and sloth, each of which can weaken our authentic larger belonging. These interior destructive forces are augmented by other ones named by modern psychology. Gandhi added seven deadly social sins to the list.[1]

When these forces are denied, buried in our unconscious, and unresolved, they can be projected into the world and create threatening enemies who must be killed or fled. Much of the social conflict in the world is fed by such projection. If the forces are recognized as part of who we are, then their energy can more easily be transmuted into positive forces that serve the world's well-being.

I have seen that transmutation again and again in me and others during graced times of contemplative practice. I see the many forces moving through me; I open them into the gracious Presence and let them be accepted, calmed, released, and transformed as grace is given. I often am left with a greater sense of wholeness, of nongrasping connectedness with what is, and a sense of more freedom to respond to the needs of the world as I am called. The mystics again and again speak of the connection of knowing ourselves and knowing God. The more we truly know through our spiritual hearts the forces that shape us, the more we know as we are known by God, the more aware we become of an inclusive mutual indwelling, with our senses of call to action flowing from that awareness.

The intensity of such awareness and gifted freedom to discerningly act in the world does not usually last for long after my meditation time. However, I have found that when they are reinforced in spiritual community, in my conversations and reading, and in my own willingness, they wear better and I cannot forget their deep truth for long.

When I act in ways that contradict that awareness, I find myself less justifying of what I have done. I accept the contradictions for what they are, but I realize that they are off target blips, as a deeper part of my self remembers the larger Reality of all life happening together in God. The historic religious view of the *felix culpa*, "happy fault," shows its insightfulness as I sense that even my recognized willful acts in God's forgiving hands can mysteriously lead to redemptive fruit, beyond the pain they may cause.

At the very least, such acts lead to greater *humility*, and true humility is the starting point for living into the complexity of the world's brokenness and possibilities. Humility grounds us in openness to the mysterious, loving wholeness of God rather than in any assumed wholeness of our own knowledge. Such a virtue can free us from the temptation to think we can have a complete, final knowledge of any social situation. Further, it allows us not to think we *have* to have such complete knowledge in order to act. We can trust that God's Spirit weaves its way through what we do, showing us any crookedness in our path and opening a way to realign it with the needed path of love.

We need to learn what we can about a situation to which we feel called to respond, but our knowledge is contingent on what has been given us; there is always more to know than we know. When we keep turning to God's Wholeness rather than to an arrogant assumption of our self-sufficient knowledge, we remain open to the further knowledge we may be given as we go along. This leads us to considered actions in the world, considered by what our minds can know, by what our spiritual hearts intuitively reveal to us, and by the challenges of what others say. Such actions can be energetic and firm based on the knowledge we have. At the same time, they can be carried out in a way that keeps the eye of the heart open for what more we may be shown.

A Contemplative Glance at Three Social Arenas

I have chosen a few widely diverse social situations where I can illustrate the perspective contemplative awareness can bring to the global human struggle for mutual well-being. Each of them has a tremendous impact on human community at various levels. The first addresses social violence, with a special focus on war. Then I turn to the interpersonal arena of erotic passion. Finally, I bring our attention to the ways we relate to the Earth.

WAR AND THE QUEST FOR FULLER LIFE

The more complex the area of social calling, the more considered our actions need to be. Take, for example, the long war in Iraq. A continuing stream of books and articles has shown what an ill-conceived, half-blind, and tragically destructive war that has proved to be. This is not the place to go into varying historical emphases of what may be a just war, but I will hold up one emphasis that is particularly relevant here: the uncertainties of what may come from an act of war, together with the history of the unpredicted horrors and innocent deaths, disruptions, impoverishments, and duration of war, can outweigh any injustice being considered as a reason for war. This means that we need to enter the consideration of war with a presumption against it.

Add to this Jesus's emphasis on and example of peacemaking and loving our enemies, and the weighting against going to war (doubly so regarding a preemptive war) is profoundly supported. The contemplative Jesus realized the world's interwovenness in divine Love. He showed us the implications of that, including the need to widen our exclusive circles of identity to include others and the need for forms of compassionate action flowing from a sense of mutual belonging and receptive listening in God.

Thus, in relation to the war in Iraq (as in Afghanistan and in relation to any other form of conflict), we're called both to the humility of our limited knowledge and to active witness to what a contemplative consciousness shows us of our mutual belonging. The humility need not weaken any necessary defensive action. In fact, over time the humility serves the action. It allows us to act with openness to further knowledge that will contribute to shaping our action ever more realistically and constructively for the immediate and long-term situation.

Further, our open awareness allows us to act on behalf of our opponents as well as ourselves, because there are no ultimate enemies shown in a contemplative consciousness. We seek to hold up our mutual belonging even as we resist others' harmful actions. If we cannot do that and our goal is to vanquish our enemies and expect peace to follow, in time we will be defeated. Those who have been vanquished and held down (or their successors) will live in resentful suppression, gearing up for the day when they in turn can become the victors. That is the historical rhythm of social conflict when winning rather than reconciliation is the ultimate goal.

So, a humble confidence in divine Love, an inclusive sense of community, and acceptance of a calling to act for a just peace in accordance with our circumstances are in the long run a far more effective combination in resolving social conflict than an arrogant confidence in our power to control others, a narrow, exclusive sense of community, and action whose ultimate aim is the destruction of a perceived enemy and the arbitrary imposition of our cultural and political values. We have tasted the bitter fruits of the latter course in Iraq. Each of us who believes this needs to be open in prayer to let emerge the particular shape of our own called-for ways of supporting a better vision than the one that brought us into this war and the one that keeps us in Afghanistan.

A more hidden contribution of contemplative awareness to the arena of war is the alternative it can provide to what I would call the spiritual attraction of war. War can be felt by some people, consciously or unconsciously, as a chance to be fully alive and in an intimate exclusive community. Especially when people are involved in a defensive war, as in World War II, they are galvanized into an intimate national community that can transcend differences. In the face of war's unpredictable life-and-death realities, they may feel fearful and yet at the same time strangely more alive than before the announcement of war, just as people can feel more alive when they face individual life-and-death and other disorienting situations apart from war.

In war something big is happening. Whether or not we agree with its necessity, we can't ignore its impact. Many people are being asked to sacrifice their comforts and lives for something beyond themselves. I very much respect the willingness of so many people to sacrifice for the protection of their homeland. The power of a state of war, though, for some people can stretch beyond that motivation. Sacrifice can expose what previously may have been petty concerns and unadventurous lives. For all the dangers and changes involved in their way of life, such people may feel that this is a chance to really live into something vibrant together that transcends what may be their more constricted little world.

In such a time of disruption some people may vaguely sense the possibility of a breakthrough in their individual and public lives. Along with their fear of what may happen, somewhere inside they may hope for something new: new justice, new aliveness, new strength, new community, or new challenge. They feel that now they and the nation can forget all the patient diplomacy, nonviolent measures, and slow movement of things in normal times. At some unconscious level, they may hope that in war they can explode their way into new possibilities through the destruction of declared enemies. In moments when the inner voice full of fear and revulsion is quiet, they may sense that war just might bring greater freedom and happiness to them and others in the end, which will compensate for war's destructiveness.

If we sense such a transcendent personal and social promise in war, we may be brought to the brink of spiritual attraction to it. We cross the line from a vague sense of the war's promise into conscious spiritual attraction if we come to believe that God's Spirit has brought the war into being in order to fulfill a transcendent purpose and that God is on our side, opposing the evil spirit guiding the other side. In churches and other religious bodies we rightly pray for our troops and their families, but much more rarely do we extend the prayer to include the troops and civilians on the other side, who may tacitly be seen as in the hands of Satan or other evil forces, or at least as people less worthy of concern.

A powerful tribalism can take us over, a sense of sacred divine destiny, which we see flaring up again and again in American and world history (and in the stories of scripture itself). This is compounded if the dominant culture conditions us to value violence as a solution to differences on many levels. It's worth noting that in many nonliterate societies the word for "human" is restricted to members of the tribe. In war we often see derogatory names coined for the nations, ethnic groups, and social movements on the other side. The world is simplistically divided into light and dark, us and them, good and evil.

Looking at the full range of civilian and military experience in wartime, the stretching personal experiences and actions during a war can deepen some people's relation to God, life, and one another. In some cases they might at least temporarily lead to more just societal structures and leaders. However, such potential goods finally come at the expense of other members of God's family, often at the special expense of a great many innocent and poor people and children, to say nothing of the environment. Amid war's deceptions, disruptions, and brutalities, war also can lead to the destruction or warping of our relation to God and one another and to lifetime psychic scarring. God's redemptive hand can open the way for us again in time, but a terrible price will have been paid.[2]

So where else can we turn for fuller life and hope that's more powerful than the allure of war or other forms of collective violence? Where can we take the desire that rises in us for participating in life to the fullest, right up to the revelatory edge of death?

I would like to suggest that the graced times of contemplative practice and awareness draw us to the very source of that restless fire that drives us. Jesus said that he came to give us abundant life and joy. Moses exhorted us to choose real life in God. St. Irenaeus declared that the glory of God is a human being fully alive. Whenever we are truly in the fire of radiant Love, we touch life's fullness. In contemplative openness we are exposed to the source of such abundance.

The great mystics know that. They and many others like them in ordinary life situations are the models, the heroes, the saints, the spiritual warriors who live out that awareness in the ways they deal with human differences and situations that are life-giving for everyone. They need to be held up worldwide as pointers to the way of fuller life in community that counters the sirens of war and other forms of violent conflict.

A range of contemplative practices, as well as practices of compassionate intercession and action, especially in the context of spiritual community, can be offered as ways into that fuller life. Such ways express our desire to be disposed to the enlivening and purifying power of the divine Fire. That power stretches us toward the peaceable kingdom (kin-dom), the authentic shalom of God.

A poignant example of how the power of that enlivening Fire can be extended right to the end of life is seen in the dying days of a teacher of mine, Thomas Hand, a great modern Jesuit priest and Zen Master. When he found out that he had only a few months to live in the face of his cancer, he told a close friend that he was so looking forward to this last brief period of his life to see what would be given, what would unfold day by day. His physical dying was in the context of his deep, trusting contemplative living, the great aliveness of his practice and graced awareness.

I once spent eight days in an intensive silent Zen Christian retreat with Tom. At the beginning of that time he spoke of another kind of dying: the kind to which Jesus referred when he spoke of our needing to die in order to really live. Tom firmly exclaimed to us: "Your sitting cushion in this room is your Calvary. Here you must die."

In these vignettes from Tom's life we see the intimacy of life and death and the willingness to come to the end of what we hang on to in this life in order to rise to the further liberated life promised us. We see something of the paschal mystery of dying and rising lived out by Christ and lived by us. In the fullness of any contemplative practice, we are exposing our willingness to release that which is narrow, stale, hooked, false, and willful. We're willing to lay down our self-images and attachments, to let all pass, as we trustingly wait in the incubator of our open presence for more of the real life and calling that is ours in God.

When we catch even a whiff of that Reality, we know we're touching home. Its fruit is a quality of freedom for the real, the living, the loving in life. That's the contribution of deep spiritual awareness to all seekers after real life. It enlivens us and lights up our vision and energy for the world's well-being. It's that sacred, vibrant home ground from which we can enter the fray of God's shalom-shaping in the world in the ways we are particularly called and from which we can trustingly leave this life.

Authentic contemplative practice and awareness can help give discerning context and greater freedom from attachment to any attractions we may have to the god of war, as well as to anything else that promises fuller life than it can deliver or sustain. This discerning freedom is especially important when the price of such attachment is the demonizing and destruction of other human kin. We can resist attackers yet at the same time know that ultimately we are kin and eventually need to move toward reconciliation.

Contemplative awareness reminds me of Pogo's great line: "We have met the enemy, and he is us." The deepest enemy is our need to create an enemy, a scapegoat upon which we can hang our troubles and seek redemption through its destruction. The deeper Reality is the loving image of God mirrored among all of us, a mirroring of the divine nature that we see so powerfully in the way Jesus approached his death. Living from awareness of this depth Reality can help to check the temptations of war and of violent conflict in general. It points us to the sacred ground of true aliveness and inclusive community, the ground that the world so desperately needs to embrace together.

PRACTICES THAT CAN ASSIST OUR IDENTIFICATION WITH OTHERS

You may want to include in your spiritual practices one that concretely helps to draw out your sense of identification with our inclusive human family in God. Here are a few possibilities, which you can modify as you may be moved:[3]

1. In your prayer ask to be shown any person or group whom you identify as an enemy, someone or some group you might shun, fear, or hate. When any such enemy appears, you can say to God: "Help me to see how this person (or group) suffers." That might help you to soften your sense of an enemy, replacing it with a sense of compassion and perhaps forgiveness, even as you may remain firm in your sense of resistance to anything destructive in their behavior.
2. When people (or other sentient beings in nature) arise in your consciousness, especially any who seem alien to you, say to yourself, "This too is I" or "This too is an image of God" or "I'm looking in a mirror."
3. Trusting that the heart of God is Love, invite that Love to directly live through you—God's eyes in your eyes, compassionately seeing anyone who may come to mind.
4. As you slowly breathe in, let compassion fill your whole being. As you slowly breathe out, let that compassion flow into the world, into people or places of suffering

that appear in your mind. Be open for anything that may be inspired in you concerning your particular place in the alleviation of suffering, including the suffering and roots of war.

5. If you're open to the cross as an icon of the divine Presence, you can sit before one, preferably one with a corpus on the cross. Let that sacrificial Love seep into your spiritual heart, deeper than any words or prayers that may flare up during the time. After a while, let any other kind of suffering in the world spontaneously come to mind, including people in the midst of war, and open it to the larger Love. In the light of that Love, perhaps you can face into the world's suffering more fully and find inspiration for your place in the bearing and alleviation of that suffering.

6. Besides such meditation practices you may be moved to learn the practice of aikido. This is a martial art created by a Japanese man who felt the need for a defensive physical form that didn't hurt or kill an attacker, but would aim at protecting the attacker in the process of one's defense. The attacked person accepts the assailant's energy and blends with it while maintaining an attitude of fearless, compassionate presence, including willingness to bear the knife, club, or fist of the attacker if it comes to that, thereby not creating an internal sense of a feared enemy who must be destroyed. Through ways of quickly stepping aside from the attacker, the assailant's aggressive, off-balance energy is diverted, usually leaving them sprawled on the floor, but safe.

The practice sometimes can be extended to verbal attacks as well, where you can maintain an attitude of connectedness with the person and willingness to hear what they say, while at the same time mentally stepping aside from their attacks.

EROTIC PASSION AND FULLER LIFE

We are magnetically charged beings, made from and for connections. As embodied spirits we're potentially attracted to any other form of embodiment that shows itself—animal, vegetable, or mineral! We fall in love in many ways, through what our senses bring to us. Most people, of course, are particularly drawn to other human beings. Erotic human relationships stretch far beyond genital sexual arousal to all the ways we are drawn to be with other people. Those relationships are marked by such things as yearning for union, forms of genital and nongenital communion and companionship, volatility, inspiration, ecstasy, creative and destructive outcomes, and so much more. Together they define much of human living, literature, art, and film.

How does this built-in eros relate to our built-in attraction to the mysterious Wellspring of life that we call God? No one in my experience has better described that relationship from a contemplatively grounded standpoint than the late Shalem Institute psychiatrist Gerald May. Here is a very brief selection of his insights:

> Eroticism is in the last analysis a manifestation of the energy of divine love that has been differentiated into a certain form....We must look at it in terms of confused manifestations or expressions of the same kind of love....The writings of Christian mysticism are filled with [erotic/sexual] terms....On the other side, popular descriptions of human romance rely just as heavily on terms that are deeply spiritual,...showing just how related spiritual and sexual communion can be in our feelings.
>
> The self-centered aspect of ego will substitute erotic experience for unitive experience. Whenever possible, it will divert the flow of spiritual passion into erotic outlets. And often, after its defenses have failed and

unitive experience has occurred, the ego will prompt one to seek out eroticism as a way of re-establishing that "I can still feel sure of who I am"....In general, erotic love bolsters the strength and importance of one's self-image.

Spiritual seekers are bound to have numerous episodes in which they invest *erotic* [emphasis added] needs in God and seek to satisfy *spiritual* [emphasis added] needs through erotic interpersonal relationships. This confusion is not limited to intentional spiritual seekers. Everyone, regardless of religious or spiritual orientation, is subject to the same confusion. In fact, those people who deny any conscious spiritual longing are probably the most likely to be seeking unconditional love through their relationships with other people.[4]

We see in this complex, confused, union-seeking situation of people with one another and God a yearning to be that "human being fully alive." Let me suggest two major contributions of the fuller life afforded by contemplative awareness to our understanding of erotic passion.

1. Contemplative awareness involves a firsthand sense of profound intimacy of all forms of life with one another, rising from the same divine Wellspring. Communion— and, in its most graced dimensions, union—is seen to already exist. Thus, the erotic yearning in us is for the realization of what already is, were we conscious of it. If we can trust the historical witness of contemplative adepts about this and Jesus's declaration of our mutual indwelling in John's Gospel, then we could respond to the yearning in us differently. Instead of it being a sign of our outsideness from God, the yearning could be seen as

a sign of the communion that already exists, drawing our awareness and living out of that Reality ever further. When our consciousness is graced with a direct apprehension of that Reality, we know an aliveness that leaves us fulfilled, however temporarily. Every dimension of our being is at home in radiant Love during such times, at home deeper than any images or feelings that may accompany the apprehension.

2. This experience is authenticated by its overflow into human (and other earthly) relationships. We may recognize our soul connection with others and its divine Ground more readily, leading us to a natural compassion for them. We may find ourselves appreciating the beauty of people and things without being driven to possess them physically, because we already possess richness in God that encompasses all of life.

In appreciation, as in compassion, there is an open quality of presence in which we are engaged but not consumed by the person or object appreciated. We are left free simply to appreciate the beauty we see just as it is, letting it be. The energy in us is alive but calm, willing to enjoy the beauty, to participate in it in that way, without the need to possess it on the physical plane.

Such a quality of presence will likely leave us more free to touch the mysterious larger beauty that led St. Augustine in his *Confessions* to name God as "Beauty" in his famous postconversion prayer that begins: "Late have I loved You, O Beauty so ancient and so new…." Beauty, like authentic love, is a quality of divinity in which we can participate yet our egos cannot possess. Beauty must be free to be itself in order to maintain its own integrity. When in our minds we turn beauty into a commodity to possess, it loses its iconic power. It is reduced to an object to be taken, to be domesticated and controlled by our minds. When beauty is allowed to keep its integrity, we are humbled in wonder. The wonder can draw us to the infinite radiant Mystery that is delicately revealing itself in the beauty we see and that St. Gregory of Nyssa said is seen in us: "You have become beautiful by coming close to my Light."[5] Such thoughts raise the stakes for our times of choice between sheer appreciation of someone/something and our attempts to own them/it.

Thomas Merton spoke well to the larger spiritual Reality of our need to look at life in general in a nonpossessive way when he compared the situation of the soul in contemplation to Adam and Eve's situation in paradise. Everything is ours, but on the important condition that it is all given. We can neither claim nor take anything, says Merton, for as soon as we try to take something as if we owned it, we lose our Eden.[6]

Our awareness of divine communion brought into a committed human love relationship may soften the temptations of possessiveness by the way divine Love has shown itself to us: as tender, mutually indwelling, appreciative relationship. As these qualities come to be the central marks of the relationship in its sexual and other aspects, the couple reflects the blessed gift that a mature love relationship can be. That love is a unique expression of a larger Love to which both belong.

However, as Gerald May says, erotic sexual communion itself retains a quality of difference from *agapic* communion—that is, unconditional divine Love:

> The first-hand realization of agape demands union and, thereby, a temporary suspension of self-definition. Erotic love does not require this. [It] consists of an active, self-defining investment of one's energy and attention in another person.…"Losing oneself" in orgasm constitutes a state of highly restricted but often quite alert awareness.…In contrast, the experience of union is characterized by sharpened, clarified, *unrestricted* awareness.…The world does fall away in the

ecstasy of erotic love at the moment of orgasm and at many other moments of total preoccupation with one's lover. In contrast, the ecstasy of agapic love is characterized by an awesome joining *with* all the rest of the world, becoming a part of it.[7]

Hopefully, though, the taste of direct communion with God brought to the human relationship can soften this distinction and allow human love to connect us with the world more fully.

It's worth mentioning here the experience and practices of major Asian contemplative traditions related to eros. They have a long history of seeing erotic energy as a dimension of a larger energy in us that can be manifest in many forms. The genital sexual manifestation of this energy is good, but it can become a fixation hindering the energy from being transmuted into larger dimensions of human/spiritual aliveness, especially compassion and enlightenment. Those traditions teach many practices meant to lighten the genital intensity of the energy and free it to become more available for other dimensions of communion that are called for at a given time.[8]

Part of my God-given freedom is to choose whether to let the forms of energy in me, as I interact with others, take me toward a truly alive spiritual presence that reveals my deepest humanity in God and appreciative kinship with others or toward an illusory or surface aliveness expressing a narrowly driven, possessive quality of presence. Part of my unfreedom is seen in the ease with which I can be overwhelmed by the power of that energy as it becomes narrowly attached to a particular person or object.

In such a time, I want to invite the Spirit's empowering presence to transmute that trapped energy into a true, liberating quality of being alive, of moving in whatever direction is called for. That direction may well be toward physical expression in a committed relationship of love. However, the energy's movement then will likely be less driven and possessive and more simply appreciative and self-giving. Such nonattachment, allowing free, available energy for the necessary direction of real love, is an ancient exhortation in one form or another found in Christian and many other spiritual traditions.

NATURE'S BODY, GOD'S BODY

Let me hold up one other arena of community and see what a contemplative consciousness can contribute: our community with nature. This arena is critically and universally in need of attention today if we and the Earth are to survive and thrive.

As a global community we are just beginning to seriously wake up to the devastating price of our increasing disconnectedness from the Earth's well-being and its inhabitation by God's Spirit. Since the beginning of the Industrial Revolution people have increasingly moved from the countryside to cities, where nature is more remote and more controlled by human forces. We have increasingly treated nature as other than us. We have homed in on Genesis 1:28 as a mandate to rule the Earth's creatures as one huge, inert commodity field to exploit for the needs and wants of human consumption and financial profit.

In doing so we ignore the prophetic vision of Isaiah 11:6–9 and 65:25 and the Psalmist's call to see God's glory in this living universe. Isaiah's vision of the New Jerusalem, as Robert Morris well says,

> speaks of an animal-human connection opened up by human alliance with the unifying wisdom of life, which flows like God's breath through the earth.... The vision claims to be rooted in the very heart of God. The world is seen working as the Creator knows it can work. And humans are invited into the heart of the vision so that we can experience a heart-changing

metanoia, a turning around in the way we build the earth.[9]

God has too often been placed in a transcendent heaven with little direct connection to nature since Earth's creation, except as nature has a supporting role in the drama of human history. We have been taught an anthropocentric rather than a biocentric universe, although we still see vestiges of biocentric awareness in the cosmological stories and practices of ancient cultures.

We all benefit from the ways we have learned to harness the forces of nature for human well-being. However, we all suffer from the way this has evolved without a sense of the Earth as a living body that births us—a body that needs not just to be used but to be cared for. That caring needs to surpass the utilitarian purposes of our material sustenance. We need a deeper purpose of loving it as our larger earthly parent, which means loving it as part of God's creation, appreciating its mysterious beauty and appreciating the way it sustains and interacts with us. We also need other people and organizations that can inspire and help us to discern how to act out of that love.

Many current theological books and articles take a fresh look at scripture and the spiritual tradition in ways that more fully affirm human and divine connectedness to the Earth.[10] These writings, in effect, advocate the Earth's resanctification in human consciousness. They often ground us in the Genesis story of our creation from the dust of the Earth, animated by the divine Breath. Many of the authors draw us to reverence the Earth along with ourselves as a gift of divine creation. They show us what it means to share in the sustenance of its life-giving cycles, knowing not only the intrinsic value of these cycles but also our dependence upon them.

As Brian Swimme and Thomas Berry have written, scientific knowledge shows us that we live not only within the life cycles of earthly nature but also within a cosmic history of irreversible transformations. This history is a kind of drama, a shared great story of evolution, which belongs to us all. Swimme and Berry go so far as to say that this new consciousness is equivalent to a new religious tradition, as we come to see the universe itself as a type of revelatory experience.[11]

The Earth and all creation can be seen as part of God's cosmic body. Our most broadly shared divine-human-creation covenant can be seen in the Genesis creation story. Humans have a distinctive place in a much larger and mysteriously blessed community of creation. As Swimme and Berry explain, we can update that story today by including the astrophysicist's/cosmologist's more precise understanding of the birth and ongoing evolution of creation, which is part of our common story.[12]

Those scientists and theologians who have taken this story seriously have expanded our personal identity to include the "family" of galaxies, energy fields, and all the rest of what we're coming to know about creation. We're a distinctive part of a symbiotic cosmic community. Physically, we're literally made of stardust. The fifth-century mystic Denys the Areopagite, whose influential writings can be seen as the culmination of the bridging of Greek Neoplatonism and the Christian mystical tradition, would understand this. Denys said that because of their unity of origin all things are bound together in the intimacy of "friendship."[13]

St. Francis of Assisi's famous "Canticle of the Creatures," which includes Brother Sun and Sister Moon, gives us a powerful example of a mystical saint whose spiritual awareness drew him to an integral sense of belonging to the family of creation. We see this in Jesus's experience in the wilderness with the wild beasts, in other times of his withdrawal to pray, and in his appreciation of God's care for the lilies and the birds. The very essence of holiness, of participating more fully than others in the Wholeness of God, often includes an intimate life with nature beyond our own humanity. Isaac of Syria affirms this when he says that the sign of a fully merciful heart is when it burns with love for all creation.

Gerald May chronicled his profound personal experience of the wisdom and healing power found in the wilderness in his last book, completed just before his death.[14] The great twelfth-century contemplative St. Hildegard of Bingen observed, "Prayer is nothing but the inhaling and exhaling of the one breath of the universe." Our belonging to that divine Breath means our belonging to all that is animated by that Breath, as all belongs to us.

A contemplative consciousness thus contributes direct, intuited experience of our interdependence. It recognizes that the divine, human, and environmental dimensions of life are utterly interdependent, mutually belonging—indeed, mutually indwelling. This experience powerfully complements the scientific and theological descriptions of that interdependence.[15]

In graced *ecstatic* moments of contemplative awareness, we also might sense the Earth (and, in fact, the cosmos) as a community of exaltation and joy in being, as Brian Swimme and Thomas Berry put it. They use the wonderful example of a flock of larks, which in early Modern English was called an exaltation of larks—the exaltation, if you will, of their flight, song, and sheer delight in aliveness, beyond its afflictions.[16]

Further Perspective on Contemplation in Action

Intimacy with God in every dimension of creation has social consequences. Contemplation and social action are not contradictory or even just parallel orientations. We can best speak of contemplation *in* action. Our contemplative stance at its most empowered becomes the deep, steady ground of our called-for actions, however small or great, that contribute to the world's well-being.

That stance is centered on the radiant Love that has been touched. This enlightened Love becomes the lens through which the world is seen. We're likely to become subversive of whatever is born of fear, hate, greed, and oppressive domination in the social fabric, as well as in ourselves. We become subversive because in contemplative awareness we have tasted the love that casts out fear, and the inclusiveness of creation's family in God that casts out any sense of ultimate divisions between us. We also become subversive because we've tasted something of God's richness in the moment that is overwhelmingly sufficient. We know a fullness that casts out the sense of poverty, the poverty that makes us protect and grasp for more than we need of the world's deceptively filling goods.

The gracious Love gives us motivation to care for Love's shalom in every dimension of the world's life. That Love's Spirit then moves in our spirit and shapes our particular callings to open the way for God's Wholeness in the world, however provisionally, for the kingdom (kin-dom) of God isn't a static affair: it's always growing in our midst, like a mustard seed. It's an ever-unfolding Reality revealed and lived out in the moment's grace. We can respond with great energy and steadiness yet without attachment, ever willing to change our action as we are shown what is called for now.

This detachment is aided by the contemplative practice of being present before thoughts appear, present in the open spaciousness of the spiritual heart. There Reality shows itself as it is, larger than any particular interpretations of it. When thoughts come then, they hopefully flow from that deeper awareness, but they are relative to it. They cannot contain the whole; they are ever subject to modification.

We proceed with what we're given to do in terms of action once we reach a sufficient sense of confidence in its rightness. However, we do so with humility born of awareness of the contingency of our thoughts (including our interpretations of scripture), rather than with the idolatry of frozen conceptual images to which we become attached. We continually return wide open to Reality in God before our thoughts rise, to the seedbed of our spiritual hearts where thoughts can dissolve and we are free to let new ones emerge.

The whole range of our contemplative practices can be a contribution to the world's shalom. The practices give breathing room and perspective for our culturally overstimulated and grasping minds: the freedom to "let go and know that I am God." In that process we find greater freedom to listen for what truly belongs to the way of shalom and for our part in that at a given time. Authentic contemplative practices move us away from an overly separated, ego-dominated sense of self and world. That view easily leads to an inadequate understanding of our self and the social scene and to off-target actions.

Contemplative practices hold up the wondrous intermingled grace of the moment as our true home. That means that whatever action plans we bring to the moment, we don't treat them as separate from the living Presence; we don't slip into a mental time-out from its reality. Remembering that graced Presence draws into us the spiritual oxygen needed for our authentic understanding and responsiveness to callings. Even if we can only let in a little oxygen at a given time, it will help us.

One great service of a spiritual director/companion is to facilitate our seeing and embracing what is being given us to do as individuals. When a *group* is involved in discernment, there are many ways we can help one another remain attuned to the larger creative Love present in our midst.

In our actions stemming from both our individual and group discernments, we can relate more to the evolving process of those actions than to trying to control or judge their results. The anonymous Weaver's Prayer shows us the wisdom of this: "Dear Lord, my life [we could add "church" and "society"] looks like a mess of tangled threads and knots. But that's because I only see the underside." We can be part of the weaving of shalom without knowing the outcomes but trusting the value of what's been given us to see and do at a given time.

A Practice for the Courage to Act

Hearing a call in the social arena and following up on it, even with the support of others, are two different things. That's especially true if the call involves any significant dimension of risk, time consumption, or frustration. We have a physical/psychic resource in us that can aid the special courage and energy that we need sometimes to respond to what our contemplative heart shows us is called for. It is the nerve plexus or chakra center located two finger widths below our navel. It has different names in different traditions. In the Japanese Zen Buddhist tradition, this center sometimes is called the *hara* (the broad stomach area, including intestines), or it might be called the *seika tanden* located deep inside the *hara*. It appears to be related to what we crudely call our guts, in the symbolic sense of bold courage. In the Zen tradition, it refers more broadly to a view of the unitive center of the body and psyche that realizes life whole, beyond dualisms. The full realization of that view involves posture, breathing, and mental practices found in the Zen tradition, but I am only looking at this center here as it relates to a quality of strength in us.[17]

If you are discerning a call to social action and sense the need for energetic courage to follow it, let me invite you to this version of an exercise for courage, inspired by Zen practice but adapted to the Christian contemplative context of this book:

1. Close your eyes and place your hands over your physical heart. Now lean back into your receptive spiritual heart, however you best do that.

2. Bring to God your openness to be a vessel of social compassion. See what is given you about how you are called to be such a vessel. What comes to you may be some kind of action that you're already involved in and is being confirmed, or something new may appear.

3. As such a call may show itself, see if it is accompanied by some kind of resistance—for example, a sense of doubt or a fear of getting involved or a lack of energy.

4. As any such weakening reaction shows up, bring your hands down to the center two fingers width below your navel. Push out your abdomen as you slowly, deeply, confidently breathe into that center. Continue that concentrated breathing a few times until, hopefully, you feel a sense of strength cutting through your resistant reaction to the calling—a sense of God's Strength in you. Hopefully, you're more ready, willing, confident, and energized now to move in any direction called for.

5. You can end with a prayer to be guided and sustained in your response to the calling.

We give a great deal of attention to the receptive open heart center in contemplative presence, and rightfully so. However, when we need to move beyond our resistances and gather the strength to spontaneously respond to situations that our open heart shows us, it might help if we move our attention to the *hara* center. We can see it as the God-given place in us that energizes the moving feet of the spiritual heart's call. Activating that center can help us to walk the talk, walk the calling. We can connect it with the fierce "You can do it" eye of Christ in the *Sinai Christ* icon, as opposed to his other more consoling eye. (I will say more about the eyes of this icon in the next chapter, related to leadership.)

Contemplatively Oriented Intercession

Through all of our clarity and unclarity about particular actions in terms of call and their alignment with God's Shalom, there is one particular practice that can thread its way through our time, and that is contemplatively oriented intercession.[18]

If I suspend any sense of what "I" (my little ego-self) want for myself and the world and instead let my fundamental desire be to join God in seeing and loving the world as it really is and is meant to become, which is so beyond my limited vision, then I can be openly present to God for the well-being of whoever or whatever may show itself. In such open presence, God's Spirit in me—my deepest, truest, most mysterious identity—joins God's Spirit beyond me. My limited "I" is not the center of such prayer. Nor is God, as separate from me, the center. Rather, the center is communion in God.

When I bring some particular situation or persons to such intercession, my intention is simply to share God's Love in that situation. In this process, I am recognizing that mysterious Love as the heart of reality, on behalf of whatever the particular subject of the intercession may be. I am simply present with a mind of unknowing, openly given to God's heart for the sake of this situation/person. My own desire is for whatever is most serving of creative Love, known fully by God alone. I want to be available for that Love, however that may show itself, which may be simply my offering of the situation itself at this time. Quakers, in their own way, might see this to be the gist of "holding someone (or some situation) in the Light."

An extension of such prayer is a stance in the world of holding all sides together in a given situation involving conflict. Sometimes that's our primary calling: just to hold all sides together in prayer, wanting the best way of loving action to show itself through the differences, and for that way to be recognized and followed together. At other times we may be called to move in a very particular direction on some issue, and that may cause resistance from those who disagree or don't understand what we're doing. Our prayer then can be the expression of our hope to join God's way through our action and our willingness to remain open to new light for our path of action.

This kind of prayer also maintains a sense of inclusion of those who oppose us, a desire for them to listen with us for Love's way, a sense of their belonging to the same community in God, with whom reconciliation eventually needs to happen. Such prayer participates in the outstretched arms of Christ on the cross, enfolding and inviting the whole world into reconciling Love.

PART III

Contemplatively Grounded Leadership

CHAPTER 6

Qualities of Contemplatively Grounded Leaders

Contemplatively oriented spiritual leadership happens when our acts arise from our desire to be led by the Holy Spirit. It happens when we're willing to lean our mind back into our open spiritual heart, even for an instant, as the first step of discernment and action.

Three Special Qualities of Contemplatively Oriented Leadership

Each of us is clothed in particular designated positions of spiritual leadership at different times. These positions may include specifically spiritual or religious positions, such as pastor/rabbi, chaplain, spiritual director, retreat or prayer group leader, religious educator, or church committee member, or they may also include more general positions where spiritual leadership may be called out at a given time, as in parenting, marriage partnering, friendship, teaching, counseling, management, health care, and many other work and community positions. Finally, we can find ourselves in informal moments with any person or group, where we find the Spirit calling us to say or do something related to them. Let me single out three qualities of spiritual leadership among many other possible ones that can emerge from a contemplatively grounded life.

INDEPENDENTLY ENGAGED

By *independently engaged* I mean that in our various designated spiritual leadership positions and other roles we are willing to be free for the living truth and call that the Spirit presents in the moment. We are willing to identify with God's free Spirit as the real heart of our own being. We can pray that the Holy Spirit releases us from dependence on our small self-identity, our conditioned sense of the centrality of our ego-identity and security. As that release is empowered, we are shown our deeper identity, security, and freedom in the Gracious One. Our deep identity in the image of God participates in divine strength, love, and wisdom.

As we likely all know from experience, such participation is erratic, due to our often confused and sometimes willful little self-centeredness, reinforced by our culture in so many ways. Because of that awareness we may hesitate to say or do what's come to us, fearing that what's come is ego-born. When such hesitation appears, it can be helpful to take a minute to simply lean your mind openly into your spiritual heart, wanting whatever is truly called for. Then let whatever you say or do flow from that openness as best you can.

The graced freedom to come from a deeper place might show itself, for example, when we're with a person or group and we suddenly sense the empowered call to say or do something challenging that brings fresh and needed spiritual perspective to the situation. We're able to do this even as we know that we may be left very alone on the human level because of the ego threat it might pose to those who hear it, no matter how gently we may have spoken. We have said something that does not bolster people's individual or collective little self-centeredness.

What has come through us one way or another points to divine Love itself as our true center. That Love calls us in some particular way to let go our holding on to an overly separated and narrow sense of self as the center. Many of our contemplative practices are meant to condition us to be present in the immediate self-less openness before a narrow sense of self clicks in.

When we're free in such independent engagement, we find ourselves grounded deeper than our desire to please the people we're with and deeper than our desire to secure ourselves. We're at home in God's Love, and we trust that we can bear any of the consequences of our words or actions that have been inspired by that Love. In such moments of prophetic spiritual leadership, we're living from the same place in which Jesus lived when he said, "Perfect love casts out fear." In such gifted times, enlightened Love has shown itself as the true Wellspring of our being.

When we're graced with real confidence in what's given us in such moments, we might even find ourselves with a sense of delight rather than just the tightness of holding our breath in preparation for what may be the reaction of others. We've been graced to go deeper into the fuller divine Reality and call of the moment. We're happy to be free from our ego-created straightjackets that would suppress such a call. We feel more real and alive. We have shown spiritual leadership; that is, we have let the Spirit lead through us.

So, difficult as it may be, our deep grounding in the moment as it is in God can have a way of freeing God's hand through us in challenging and needed ways. In such graced moments we know what it is to be in the world but not of it; in the situation but not finally dependent on its ego dynamics; in the situation but of God. In such graced times, we are indeed independently engaged spiritual leaders.

DISCERNINGLY FLEXIBLE

In the last practice described in chapter 5, I spoke of praying with an icon called the *Sinai Christ*, a full-faced image of Christ. Many people have noticed that each of the powerful eyes of this icon seems quite different. In my own experience I have found one of the eyes to be very pastoral and supportive. It's as though God's Spirit in Christ accepts all my sins and limitations and lets me know that I am loved through and beyond them. Indeed, if I am made of Love, made of God's Love-energy, how could it be otherwise? Love is seeing itself reflected in my form, in my unique coloration of Love.

The other eye, though, shows a different quality. To me it has a penetrating, fierce, energizing presence, as though Christ is seeing God's transforming Spirit in me. I'm being shown that I'm capable of doing many things for the shaping of the divine Shalom in the power of the living Spirit. I can let the Spirit stretch me beyond where I am. This eye energetically says, "Buck up, my Spirit is mingling in your spirit. You can do it!"—whatever the called for "it" may be. The other eye says, "You are loved (or, more precisely, You are intrinsically part of Love), even when you can't or don't do it."

I'm always left with the sense that I need to let both eyes of the icon open my spiritual heart, as each is needed. I always tell people, by the way, that if they ever pray with this icon, they can sense for themselves which eye is which. In a sense there's no right answer to that, only the one that we individually experience, and our experience may change in different times before the icon. When we're opening ourselves to the living "far-nearness" of God through the icon, as in all authentic prayer, we find ourselves involved in a dynamic, evolving relationship.

It's interesting to note how these two complementary qualities of presence can be separated into two different kinds of leaders. In certain Japanese Zen monasteries, it's traditional to have two leaders, one of whom is stern and stretching of the monks, the other of whom is gentle and supportive. I'm sure such a division of leadership spontaneously or intentionally happens in many other monasteries, as well as in families, congregations, and many other contexts. These instances become a confirmation of the human need for both qualities.

For us as informal or designated spiritual leaders, there is often a particular sequence in receiving the message of the icon's eyes. Those of us who have steady roles with people—for example, as spiritual directors, pastors, or parents—can seem very predictable and reassuring to others. We reliably show up for those we are to be with, and we symbolize for them a securing spiritual Reality. We're there for them. We pray with them. We want them to realize God's liberating Love. That accepting, caring eye of Christ is there for them through us.

When people have evolved a certain trust of that Love, they become freer to receive the penetrating eye that yearns to melt away defensive fear, illusion, willfulness, and apathy. People then can become more open to the called-out invitations to a more truly God-centered, risk-taking, and joy-filled life in the Spirit, in the particular circumstances of their lives. They can more easily embrace their desire for the unique image of God in them to shine brightly and freely.

When we're with people over time in some spiritual capacity and they have come to a foundational sense that God is for them and in them, we find ourselves involved in an ongoing spontaneous discernment as to which eye we are called to show them at a given time. We need to be willing to be moist clay in God's hands in these situations, to borrow the imagery of St. Irenaeus, with a desire to see people with whichever eye is needed now. We need to be discerningly flexible.

INNOCENT ARTIST

St. Paul calls us "God's work of art" (Eph 2:10). Being shaped in the image of God, we continue the creative life of the divine Artist. Contemplatively grounded artist leaders are innocent artists, because what creatively comes through our leadership rises out of the virgin soil of our vulnerable listening silence—out of our openhearted presence. We enter the silence ultimately shorn of all we know with which we would clothe and protect ourselves and others. We enter the silence in trust that something will be shaped through us that shimmers with a light that is more than our own.

The fruit of this innocent artistry need not be something dramatic. It may be what comes to us for the design of a contemplative prayer session; or for a new dimension of congregational, community, or workplace ministry; or for an imaginative response to a spiritual directee's or child's or fellow worker's question. Whatever comes, it comes as a surprise to us, because it arises from the fertile darkness of an innocent heart. That heart carries nothing but its desire for God's artistry to show itself as it will.

As with all true art, whatever comes forth will carry its own authentic message and beauty, however simple or sophisticated it might be. It will inspire a truth or action or appreciation that someone needs to embrace but has difficulty seeing without the spiritual artist's medium of grace.

What comes to be shared may be very serious or hilariously funny. Humor can make so many truths more digestible. Someone once said that it is humor that allows us to tell people the truth without being killed by them for having done so!

Being an innocent artist, as with the other qualities of contemplatively grounded spiritual leadership, involves a trustworthy sense of the larger loving Presence alive within and among us. When we're willing, or at least when we *want* to be willing, to let go of attachment to our own conditioned images of how things should be and what we must do and to let go of any need for an impressive personal "signature," spaciousness arises wherein God's Spirit alive in our spirit can rise up and surprise us with its creative artistry.

Other Qualities of Contemplatively Oriented Leadership

Here is a list of some other qualities of spiritual leadership, named by participants in Shalem programs, that especially connect to contemplatively oriented leadership and complement the three that I have spelled out in more detail:

- Knowing and trusting from the spiritual heart.
- Unselfconsciousness.
- Presence in God, in the moment; presence to what is in the here and now and to what is called for. A quality of discerning presence is more important than knowledge and skills.
- Honoring the image of Christ in others and in yourself.
- Accepting you where you are, allowing yourself to relax and bloom.
- Knowing that you are beloved; attentive to God in you; capable of drawing out your deepest self.
- Centered vulnerability.
- Humility that accepts your own imperfect knowledge and love and that honors the larger cloud of witnesses in the spiritual tradition.
- Willingness to engage in loving, generous, and, where called for, sacrificial action.
- Capable of articulating spiritual depth in understandable ways.
- Not confined to existing structures.
- A burning desire for a loving, wisdom-receiving, authentic relationship with the divine, for yourself and for the world.

- A confidence in the goodness of spiritual Reality and what you are doing that evokes trust but is not arrogant.
- Not in a hurry; patient.

When you read this list you can truly feel humble. Who is worthy? However, if you look at such qualities as qualities of the moment, qualities that show themselves at particular times when they are needed, then everyone who truly seeks to live from their deep self in God will find moments when they have found the grace of such qualities showing themselves.

The Second Vatican Council's document *Lumen Gentium* declares that everyone is called to holiness (§11).[1] In our broken world, holiness for most of us is of the moment, a moment when we're graced and willing to be present more intimately than in the other moments of lived separation from awareness in God. In such moments we may well show the kind of leadership called for, a leadership that moves from our wholeness in God in the moment to drawing others into the fragrance of that wholeness in some needed way.

CHAPTER 7

Formation Grounds for Contemplative Life and Leadership

What can be done better to develop the kind of more contemplatively grounded leadership that the religious community and world need today? I will share with you a few key things that seem foundational enough to suggest the need for a shift in perspective in the dominant ways of forming both clergy and laypeople. This shift is implicit in what I have already written about spiritual community and about the nature of spiritual leadership. I believe the Holy Spirit is moving through the church and world today in ways that are plowing deeper, fertile soil in which contemplatively oriented spiritual leadership can grow.

As I made clear in the last chapter, spiritual leadership as I am using that term is not restricted to designated religious leadership. Just as a contemplative isn't a special kind of person but everyone is a special kind of contemplative, so a spiritual leader isn't a special kind of person but everyone is a special kind of spiritual leader. Each of us is called to be a Spirit-led person who leads others when called to do so, be that in the context of the family, workplace, friendship, religious body, or community organization.

A spiritual leader is the same interiorly whether functioning in or out of a designated religious role (ordained or otherwise). The desire for, trust in, and sometimes sense of God's Presence is alive in them, however faint or buried or doubted it may be at times. When a spiritual leader carries out a designated religious role, it's done out of a sense of calling. The living out of that calling is grounded in the act of turning to the deeper Presence for guidance rather than in simply carrying out a professional, calculated duty.

For a number of years now I have seen how many more religious leaders want to be spiritual leaders in the heart of their leadership. This appears to be part of a larger movement of the Spirit in many religious communities around the world, where we see so much hunger for a more direct, living, intimate, discerning ongoing relationship with the divine among both laypeople and clergy, as well as with many people outside religious institutions. The contemplative tradition naturally rises to prominence in such a time, since it carries so much of the history, practice, and discernment of ever-deepening relationship with God.[1]

If I were to summarize what most needs to be encouraged in the shaping of a sustained spiritual leader, whether ordained or lay, I would say a willing and empowered capacity to let go of a sense of self-centered identity and, with it, relinquishing a sense of self-centered control of life as a larger identity in living radiant Love emerges. Along with that new identity comes a sense of calling and a willingness to be an icon of divine life in the world, available for whatever way that creative, bearing Love might show itself through us at a given time. Thus, the divine Spirit interacts with human spirit, shaping a listening and responsive mind-in-heartedness. In the context of spiritual community, this interaction expands to a "Spirit moving among us" awareness.

The Place of Education

What kind of education (in its root sense of *educare*, to "draw out"—to draw out what is true) is needed to form an ordained or lay spiritual leader? That is, how do people in intentional spiritual communities and with particular educational assumptions and methods contribute to the formation of a spiritual leader?

First of all, at their best our educational encounters can contribute to the formation of a whole, spiritually aware person, the fruit of which is availability for Spirit-leadership. This formation begins at birth in the way members of the family, by word and action, can be icons of the Spirit-Love in them, drawing out the Spirit-Love in the heart of the child. The formation continues through every significant relationship and encounter that the child has with people and nature, where there is something conveyed of the presence and "leadership" of creative Love within these shaping times. Part of the formation includes encounters with the cruelty and injustice of others that hide the Love, and with the mysterious destructive forces of natural calamities and death. Over time, hopefully, we are empowered to trust the Love as encompassing and deeper than these challenging forces.

Education in the Congregation

The local church naturally has a place in this formation process. For children and adolescents (as well as for adults), the liturgical, educational, mission, and fellowship dimensions of church can seek consistently to point to creative Love at the living heart of our being and encounters, including during our troubled times.

Given the confused and willful side of our gifted freedom, we can encounter the same forces of oppression from people within the church that we encounter with people outside it. Hopefully, there will be people for us in the church who don't try to justify or sidestep this dark part of their actions but instead model for us a willingness to confess their waywardness, to seek reconciliation, and to involve themselves in actions that alleviate oppressive actions and structures.

These and broader shapers of our sense of life in the Spirit may come to us in many forms. They may be church school teachers or pastors, but they may just as well be random people witnessing to something of grace in their life, offering a helping hand, trusting God through difficult situations, or just unselfconsciously sitting silently in the pew in a way that conveys a sense of connection with the larger loving Presence.

It is to be hoped that religious education teachers in our schools as well as in our catechetical programs would be open to including a contemplative dimension in their teaching, utilizing such resources as the Catechesis of the Good Shepherd, Godly Play, and the Way of the Child. On the level of adult faith formation as well, lay ministry formation and parish adult education programs would benefit from a dimension of contemplative awareness, as is offered by such resources as Companions in Christ and Centerpoint.

Beyond such group education and formation, there is the possibility of ongoing spiritual companionship/direction with someone or some group that shares our contemplative orientation. I spoke of individual and group spiritual direction previously. Here I would just emphasize that the spiritual journey over time can be full of surprises that disorient everything from our sense of God and self to our sense of vocation. Committing with other contemplatively minded people to probe the Spirit's dynamic life in us on a monthly basis can help us pay attention to the subtle happenings and invitations that are emerging in our lives. Over time these relationships can contribute to our steady depth of spiritual awareness, which in turn can contribute to the depth of spiritual awareness and leadership that we bring to the church's life and to all our other circles of relationship.

As many churches today probe for deeper spiritual grounding and leadership, it's important to accept that the many formational gifts that a contemplative orientation brings to this probing openness can take years to absorb. They cannot provide a quick fix. Over time, though, with mutual commitment a contemplative orientation can be a vessel through which the Spirit can wear down the many forces that impede spiritual depth and leadership. A shared intentional contemplative orientation and practice at its most authentic becomes subversive of whatever takes us away from a receptive, fluid presence and responsiveness to our deep being in God.

That subversion includes contemplative self-examination as well: the willingness to see how our contemplative way itself may have become subtly taken over by confused ego desires for control that skew both formational leadership and members' responses. An ongoing vigilance and humility, together with an abiding underlying desire for confidence in the real Presence, needs to be fostered. No kind of formational program has an intrinsic magical capacity to assuredly open authentic˙ spiritual Reality and transformation for us.

At its best, a formational gathering is a structure, a container, an incubator for the deepest kind of Spirit-soaked interactions in and between us. What happens in those interactions can't be controlled; it can only be given the best kind of room for honest depth that transcends the protective, grasping ego level of motivation. At their graced best, people find themselves being open to the Spirit's shaping. As the self-emptying and Spirit-filling process unfolds, they can find themselves becoming spontaneously Spirit-led leaders in many kinds of situations.

Monastic Settings for Formation

One of the practices found in the early desert mother/father tradition was the willingness of a seasoned desert elder to accept someone who might be called a novice to come and live with him (or her). This assumed that the conveyance of the qualities of spiritual awareness, practice, and leadership could not simply be taught as a body of knowledge found in a book, classroom, or church setting. Such awareness needed to be given as Jesus gave it to his disciples: in the interactions of daily life. From what we know, the desert elder did not necessarily talk much to the novice about the spiritual life. The elder just went about his daily routine of prayer, scripture, work, and all other activities of living. The novice could absorb the inner atmosphere of the elder's life. He could let himself be opened to Christ's Spirit more fully through the way the elder incarnated an orientation to life in God through everything that he did, said, and was.

The later Benedictine daily rhythm of life grew out of a desert-elder-inspired example. To this day, people in religious communities with a Benedictine Rule—both the members and their guests on retreat—are shaped especially by their ongoing participation in that rhythm of community life. Ordained leadership often was basically formed in the context of such a monastic community, and that is still true in places today. Sometimes such formation of clergy would come through an apprenticeship, including study, with a practicing parish priest/minister, which indirectly hearkens back to the desert tradition, although with parish ministry as well as personal spiritual life being the focus.

Our educational system today is much more influenced by a separate classroom learning context, especially in formal school settings (with increasing Internet supplements today). The local church as I have spoken of it is a locus for a more flexible de facto learning environment that can see the whole way of life of the congregation as the former (for better or worse) of the spiritual awareness, life, and leadership that is cultivated through that church experience. The congregation, at its best, provides a life-long, living formational context through all that it does. So, potentially, does the family, which has been well called the domestic church.

However, both the congregation and the family carry a broad array of purposes, and congregations are filled with an often transient mixture of people who are at different points in their spiritual journeys. The result is that concentrated, extended attention to spiritual formation can be very difficult to attain. Nonetheless, there are periods in people's lives when the Spirit seems to be powerfully moving, individually and sometimes collectively, and both the congregation and the family then can be vital arenas of supportive responsiveness to what is happening.

Other Places for Contemplative Life and Leadership Formation

Besides the congregation, the family, and monastic settings and beyond such spiritual and retreat centers and communities as the Shalem Institute, Contemplative Outreach, and the World Community for Meditation, let me single out for attention some other centers of religious life in terms of their potential for contemplative formation.

At their best, *church camps and conferences* for adults or children provide intensive opportunities for living, learning, and leading together that can powerfully shape people's sense of God's presence and a way of life that lives out of this sense. If this purpose became more consistently intentional on the part of leaders and participants, the potential of such places for furthering contemplative orientation and leadership could be great.

I can remember one particularly moving example of a small contemplative dimension built into the structure of a summer youth camp in the San Francisco Bay area, where I was present as a seminarian leader long ago. Every morning, after a little time for getting up and dressed, a bell would ring. This was immediately followed by silence in the entire camp, with the youth and leaders spreading out separately anywhere they wanted on the grounds. The silence lasted for at least twenty minutes, until the bell rang again.

Unfortunately, apart from a devotional booklet, there wasn't much help during that time with ways of being present or reflecting on what happened and encouraging its potential influence on the rest of the day. However, it became a window of Spirit-presence for many of the teenagers (and for me as well). My guess is that those daily twenty or so minutes were the only time of open, receptive silence in the teenagers' frenetic lives, the only time they were invited beneath the surface of ego worries, sensual stimulation, and cognitive learning to the spiritual heart's budding awareness.

Work projects organized by churches in poor neighborhoods and countries are another potentially intentional arena of formation. In such projects, the local people—often local church people—with whom the volunteer workers interact and sometimes live can become icons for Spirit-presence in many ways.

These ways include realizations about our mutual belonging in God and the need for a lifestyle that fosters community, justice, service, and prayer. If these events could include regular times of mutual silence and reflection on awareness rising out of the silence, the likely fresh intimate depth opened up together would contribute to the enduring spiritual formation and leadership of the participants. I have heard many stories of the transforming influences coming from such times of recognizing and appreciating Spirit's movements.

Such work projects also can be organized on an interfaith basis, with the special benefit of helping youth to come to know and respect one another across faith boundaries. An American Muslim, Eboo Patel, has begun a national movement, the Interfaith Youth Core, that organizes just such groups. He well says that there is a desperate need for providing youth with a serious pluralistic conditioning that counters the totalitarian youth programs of extremist groups in all traditions.[2]

Pilgrimages are another formational arena. For example, there can be overseas ones to sacred sites, such as the Holy Land, Egyptian desert monasteries, centers of Celtic Christianity in the

British Isles, the Spanish monasteries of St. John of the Cross and St. Teresa of Avila, the Italian friaries of St. Francis of Assisi, the Taize ecumenical community in France, and the ancient pilgrimage route to Santiago de Compostela in Spain. There also can be pilgrimages to impoverished places around the world, such as those selected by the Ministry of Money.[3]

American pilgrimages can be made to such places as the Chimayo healing shrine north of Santa Fe, New Mexico, various Native American centers, the shrine of the early Jesuit martyrs in Auriesville, New York, the shrine of Our Lady of Guadalupe in Mexico, places of awesome natural beauty, the shrines of particular saints, and places of historical or contemporary civil rights and other struggles for social and environmental justice.

Local pilgrimages can be organized to such destinations as memorials to saintly people who were inspiring vessels of the common good, places where people have died for a worthy cause or in innocence (like the Holocaust Museum if you live in the Washington, DC, area), and to different houses of worship on an interfaith pilgrimage.

One of the Shalem Institute's senior staff members, Carole Crumley, has been leading such pilgrimages with a contemplative heart and structure for many years. I have been privileged to be a participant or coleader for a number of these. For major pilgrimages (which can last as long as two weeks) Carole organizes pilgrims as a spiritual community: each person chooses ahead of time to take on the responsibility of a particular area of servant leadership for the group throughout the pilgrimage. Where possible, classic monastic titles are used, such as scribe, almoner, and porter, and such other positions as chaplain and spiritual director are added. Daily periods are scheduled for silence, prayer, readings relevant to the pilgrimage, and reflection on the grace being shown people along the way.

Such pilgrimages bring people together outside their normal secure habitats, with the shared intent of cultivating open presence for God and care and appreciation for one another and for God's world. Openness to carrying through this intent in all the encounters of such a vulnerable movement through unknown places can have a transformational personal and communal effect.

Many people are being further formed in their sensitivity to Spirit-presence and in the ways they show Spirit-led leadership. It is quite different from a tour of some area or travel that is labeled a pilgrimage but that doesn't really encourage and aid significant ongoing personal and communal living and leading in the Presence together.

Carole Crumley believes that an authentic pilgrimage models the emergent church that so many people hunger for today. Such a church, like a pilgrimage, shows a rhythm of learning, caring, and praying, of ecumenical community and solitude, and a transcendence of differences through a common grounding in the open spiritual heart. Both an emergent church and a pilgrimage also encourage willingness to face into new realities, challenges, and calls day by day, steeped in a hopefulness born of shared trust that God's Spirit is alive in us and the world, ever opening the way to shalom.[4]

A contemplatively oriented pilgrimage is a valuable opportunity for personal and leadership formation and envisioning that awaits discovery by more people. In the right situation it could be expanded to include a work project, and in some situations it could be made inter-generational.

Church-Related Schools and Colleges

So much of what chaplains and religious teachers are expected to do traditionally involves teaching and dialoguing with students about God and the church, leading worship/liturgical services for students, being available for counseling, and perhaps helping to organize service projects. Today we increasingly also see openness to guidance in ways to meditate and pray. If such practices could be offered with an overarching intent of bringing the mind to the heart and there learning a receptive presence to the loving Wisdom alive in and around them, then the leader could assist the weaving of contemplative awareness throughout the whole daily life of students (and interested faculty as well). Such an objective could conceivably be threaded through all the chaplain/teacher roles in various imaginative ways, as well as in the direct teaching of contemplative practices.

I'm convinced that the deeper receptive presence cultivated by contemplative practices could bring a backdrop of greater sanity to much of the inner and behavioral shared craziness of adolescence and of school and college life. Offered by the leader with a sense of providing ways of opening students to their deeply loved nature in God and to the delicate immediate presence and callings of divine Love, such practices could help them discover the confident ground in themselves that is deeper than the endless gyrations of their feelings, thoughts, and self-images.

Contemplative practices are best taught collectively in school settings in small groups or classes, with ways of encouraging availability to one another so that students who feel the need can reflect on how a practice is affecting their lives. Such encouragement would imply that they, and not just the teacher, can be Spirit-led companions for one another. If questions have been raised, what comes up in such companionship could be brought to group sessions, where the chaplain/teacher and others could become part of the dialogue.

What potentially comes of such sessions, spread over months of time, are obvious or subtle signs of the Spirit's deepening of the students' consciousness. The leader/teacher can help embed what happens in the framework of scripture and of the long contemplative tradition, whose adepts show us all kinds of shifts in our understanding of self, the world, and God, and of our sense of calling. As some members of a group of students may share some of these shifts, together they may sense a certain disconnection with some of the dominant assumptions of other students and perhaps of teachers and others as well. They may become an informal subculture of probing understanding and values, within which they can find mutual support as they encounter views and behaviors in the dominant culture that contradict what seems to be growing in them.

Some of the involved students may, in time, be called upon by others for kinds of spiritual and social leadership, which they find themselves carrying out from a deeper place of Spirit-listening and compassion than before. In such ways, the teacher's contemplative guidance may have an unpredictable multiplier effect. As I have affirmed earlier, contemplative awareness is not meant to be just a private spiritual affair. It's meant to create communities of discerning and responsive openness to the living Spirit that spill over to one another and become leaven that helps to grow the school's and world's spiritual and social well-being.

Can we go further than such groupings and dream of an entire school curriculum grounded in respect for contemplative awareness integrated with rational analysis? What might that do to the way each subject is taught? Hopefully contemplatively oriented teachers can bring Spirit-grounded imagination to such questions. The greatest challenge of a contemplative orientation to our current dominant understanding of education is the integration of mind and open awareness. A contemplative orientation isn't focused on a new metaphysical content for the mind, but on an appreciation of a different *epistemology*. It points to a more inclusive way we can know reality.

What are the implications of this way of knowing for the special formation ground of seminaries? I wrote a full treatment in answer to that question. It is available at www.shalem.org. It includes many ideas for reframing the way seminary learning and living are understood, and suggestions for mind-in-heart teaching. Many of these are transferable to other educational settings.

Conclusion

A contemplative orientation offers a badly needed way for educational institutions to move beyond overly sectarian and rational religion and overly secular and rational humanism. It can be a leaven within religious and educational bodies, between them, and between them and the secularly oriented world.

In terms of leadership, the kind of mind-in-heart formation acquired through the many grounds for contemplative formation mentioned in this chapter in turn can cultivate mind-in-heart-guided leaders for society at every level of decision making. They would be subject to normal human limitations, of course, yet at the same time, as they were true to their formation, they would be leaning back again and again into the unlimited loving Presence, wanting to be available to its movements for human well-being. The world needs many more leaders who are willing to lean back in this way and then to lean forward into the world with what has been given them.

CHAPTER 8

Exploring Further Contemplative Frontiers

I have tried to show some of the vital gifts that a contemplative orientation can bring to the deepening spiritual journey, especially to the frontiers of our spiritual understanding and practice, different levels of community, leadership, and formation. In this last section I want to briefly present a few further frontiers, ones that I leave for some of you to more deeply explore now and in the years ahead. The promise of such exploration for the world could be great, because these are frontiers (along with the ones portrayed earlier in more detail) where I believe contemplative awareness can bear much fruit. This certainly is not an exhaustive list of further frontiers where contemplative awareness can bring gifts. Many others may come to you as worthy of exploration.

Connecting with More Men

Some years ago Gerald May did some research on why so many more women than men participate in religious and especially spiritually oriented events. The many possible complicated genetic, psychological, cultural, and personal reasons for that reality are way beyond the scope of this book. Suffice it to say that men, on the whole, tend to veer more toward the exterior life. Women more readily bond and share around intimate inner experience; men tend to bond and share more through goal-oriented activities.

The pastoral role involves both attention to intimate inner experience and to goal-oriented exterior management and project development. Since the legal barriers within many denominations that prevented women from entering this historic role came down in recent decades, women have flocked to seminaries in growing numbers and have become an increasingly higher percentage of the ordained clergy in those churches. In Catholic parishes, it is often religious and lay women who serve as pastoral associates and also make up the majority of staff members at Catholic retreat and spiritual centers.

One result of women's emergence into a broad spectrum of leadership roles is that they increasingly are both the religious/spiritual leaders as well as most of the participants in congregations and spiritual/educational programs. It's wonderful to see the gifted enthusiasm of so many women in these leadership roles, as well as to see so many as participants now. But where are the men? Can the interior spiritual life be approached in a way that leads more of them to be contemplatively responsive both as participants and leaders, for their sakes and for the sake of what it could bring to the life of the world they touch? In what ways might contemplative awareness be encouraged among men?

First, many men seem to thrive in an atmosphere that has elements of teaching or mentoring rather than mutual sharing of intimate experience. This might mean that a contemplative group would be more attractive to men if it was presented as offering a body of mystical wisdom, such as teaching a particular practice and its purpose and concluding with carefully structured questions that draw out descriptions of what happened during the practice, with dialogue that seeks to relate what happened to the nature and purpose of contemplative awareness. Such an approach would minimize open-ended, unstructured silence and end-in-itself intimate sharing.

Second, many men also crave real solitude, where they can find silence, openness, appreciation, and the joy of simply being without needing to always be doing. Many of them might best find solitude in the woods or desert; while hiking, camping, or fishing; either alone or with others who don't demand more intimate sharing than they can handle. Some men would prefer to talk off the cuff sitting side by side while fishing or doing something else rather than directly facing another with an assigned task of intimate sharing.

Third, if they were gathered in a special men's group, men might feel affirmed in taking contemplative awareness seriously because they saw a lot of other men doing so. Many men may sense that they relate and respond personally and spiritually in ways that are less intuitive and more conceptual, less intimate and more objective and emotionally distant than women. If they feel that the heart of religion/spirituality requires them to be different from the way they naturally are (or have been conditioned to be), they may carry a sense of alienation or inferiority related to spiritual things. Meeting separately from women may free them to be present more on their own terms.

Fourth, men in our culture are almost completely devoid of any powerful rites of initiation into adult male spiritual life and leadership that would include an intensive process of spiritual development and the support of older men (including fathers). For many men, the result is a life that remains spiritually adrift and unresponsive to the calls for spiritual maturity and leadership.

The Franciscan Richard Rohr has sought to remedy this dearth through intensive gatherings of men who go through a serious, carefully structured process over a period of days. Participants are encouraged to share their stories honestly with one another and to participate in contemplative and reflective time alone in the desert. The huge response to his gatherings says something about the hunger of many men for a structured way into deeper spiritual awareness and living, a way that respects the often distinctive wounds and needs of men.

Fifth, many men might better respond to contemplative awareness as a spiritual path if it was presented in terms of a sense of adventure, focused exploration, and maybe even risk taking, desires probably rooted deep in the survival genes of ancient male hunter/warrior culture. In this adventure, many men might be more at home if they felt free to sense the Light in transpersonal as well as intimate personal terms. In the Hindu tradition, there is a distinction between a very affective, devotional path to the divine, full of intimate feeling and surrender to a very personal sense of God, and a more transpersonal sense of divine Reality approached through a path of structured practices and learning for the emptying of illusions and availability to the realization of transcendent Light. Many men might feel more themselves on the spiritual journey if they felt it was valid to approach God in the latter way as much as in the former.

Finally, you will recall those two eyes of Christ in the icon mentioned earlier, one that is fierce and energizing, declaring in the face of whatever your situation is, "You can do it," while the other eye offers loving support, even when you can't do it. It's the first eye that especially connects with the kind of spiritual encouragement to which many men can best respond. For many men, a respect for that place of sacred strength in which resides the risk-taking, sacrificial, potentially self-less courage in us to stay the course, to energetically say and do whatever is called for, regardless of price, may help them feel that something often sensed as so basic to their manhood has a real place in the spiritual journey, complementing the heart center's receptive, loving communion, which they also need to cultivate.

Women are of course involved in all these dimensions of choice as well. However, my purpose here has been to address ways that might help more men to join women in embracing the deeper spiritual journey more fully and authentically, ways that are especially informed by contemplative awareness.

The Spiritual Opportunities of Longer Life

Recently I read that a Stanford professor had developed an orthopedic shoe that could retard osteoporosis in the knee joint and enable people to walk for more years of their life. Part of his motivation was the realization that more and more people in many parts of the world are living longer and longer lives. Churches and other religious communities are full of people who live for decades beyond retirement. How can we also retard "osteoporosis" of the spiritual mind and heart and move to increased spiritual strength and openness in the drawn-out later years of life?

In traditional Hindu culture, life is divided into four stages, the last of which, old age, is considered the most opportune time for opening deeply to the spiritual ground of our being. In old age people would be respected who left their homes and found places of solitude, spiritual community, and simplicity of lifestyle, places where they could live more deeply into the divine Presence. Rather than being a time focused on entertainment and continuation of earlier patterns of being, behaving, and thinking, the time becomes an opportunity for spiritual reflection, practices, and compassion. This takes spiritual advantage of a period of life where people usually no longer need to focus on education, work, and the rearing of a family.

We lack such a view in Western culture, and religious centers especially need to recognize the value of such a view of aging. Instinctively, a number of spiritually sensitive older people understand this view and find themselves going on retreats, joining spiritually oriented groups, reading spiritual books, offering spiritual wisdom and practices to others as catechists, spiritual directors, retreat leaders, and so forth, and responding to calls for compassionate caring.

To really embrace a deeper spirituality in later life often requires a sense of religious legitimacy and support. The spiritual journey involves ambivalent forces in us. On the one hand, we may hear the call to move into a new stage of life and spiritual possibility. On the other hand, we may be satisfied enough with the way we've accommodated ourselves to family, cultural, and religious/spiritual life. Our spiritual lethargy, then, leaves us on a plateau where we would just as soon remain.

Often it takes an unexpected disorientation, such as the loss of someone close or some other crisis, for us to awaken to God's further invitations to spiritual realization. We then might gain enough incentive to risk losing where we are. We might let ourselves be taken to challenge the dragons that guard the door to deeper life, in order to live on the Spirit-guided frontier of our souls.

The disorientation might take another form: the loss of our familiar sense of God and faith. The contemplative tradition witnesses to such "dark nights," while at the same time affirming that the divine Presence has not left us then; we are being purified and prepared for a deeper, freer life in God. We are being drawn toward realization of union. In our consciousness God may have lost a name, and yet we may well sense the substance of divine Reality living in and around us. Defined belief has been replaced by naked trust. Such a potential disorientation needs to be recognized in churches as a valid dimension of the spiritual journey. The honest reflection of such people needs to find a place for expression and support.

A contemplative orientation can offer many older people vital practices and insights that by grace might draw them beyond what they have received through more traditional forms of Bible and theological study, prayer, and other practices.

Churches often lament having too few young people and too many old ones. Maybe there's a positive side to this reality. With older people living longer and healthier, they will have more time and, hopefully, the inclination to pursue a spiritual depth that other dimensions of their lives may have curtailed until now. New members of the church might come not only from younger people but also from other people who have become old and free enough to care about the spiritual journey in a fuller way. Such members over time could help deepen the spiritual life of the whole congregation.

Mutual Gifts of Science and Contemplative Awareness

In recent years the physical sciences as a whole have developed a much greater sense of the complexity and vastness of the universe, including the interior universe of our bodies. This awareness has led some scientists toward greater humility, with a view now that science can never answer all of life's mysteries. Many scientists, however, may well still believe that it's only a matter of time before science fills in the blanks of our knowledge of every dimension of reality. A faith-filled scientist recently said that he feels he is involved in discovering something of the mind of God in his research. I want to hold up three streams of current scientific investigation that connect with our spiritual contemplative awareness.

SPIRITUALITY AND THE BRAIN

The first stream involves new evidence that demonstrates how different dimensions of our spiritual nature are hardwired in our brains. George Vaillant, a psychiatrist and professor at Harvard Medical School, says that religious dogma, like science, lives in our thinking, analytic neocortex. Spirituality, however, resides in a different part of the brain: our limbic system. He speaks of spirituality as the positive emotions of hope, love, joy, awe, gratitude, forgiveness, and faith. These produce social connections, as opposed to emotions like fear, anger, and grief, which can isolate us from others. Religious dogma, on the other hand, as well as forms of religious observance, arises from culture. All the world's religions must be learned, but spirituality is in our genes.[1]

Even if such qualities of spiritual awareness are hardwired in our brains, their actual realization is a gift to us when they appear. We're given the activation of these qualities, and then our will, responding to the Spirit's invitations, can choose to embrace them as vital to life's purpose, or not. Vaillant does not cross the line to such a faith statement, but he does leave room for that possibility, positing that religion, at its best, helps us to live out of these positive qualities over a lifetime.

We may have a steady sense of the spiritual value of the hardwired qualities he mentions, but at the same time we may struggle with the conditioned rational interpretations of faith, especially when they seem disconnected from the depth of those innate qualities. The rational theological interpretations at their truest grow out of the theologian's and the tradition's gifted reception of those qualities and identification of them with the creative divine Presence. Theology in this sense is grounded in spirituality, grounded in the genetic spiritual capacity that God has evolved in us. Our spiritual awareness precedes and shapes our theology. Perhaps a symbol of this connection is the historical singling out of St. Paul's "faith, hope, and love" (1 Cor 13:13) as the three cardinal theological virtues.

Some other modern research seems to move in Vaillant's direction. Dean Hamer, a molecular geneticist, defines *spirituality* as the capacity for self-transcendence (including self-forgetfulness, transpersonal identification that gives us a reverence for life, and mysticism in the sense of intuitive insights not explainable by science). His research points to this capacity as partly genetically based. It is available to individuals dependent on variations in their genetic makeup. This would partly explain why we find so much diversity among the ways people connect with spirituality.[2] Another recent research project points to altruism as being hard-wired in our brains. Generosity activates a primitive part of the brain that usually lights up in response to food or sex; that is, generosity produces a sense of pleasure. It's in giving that we receive.[3]

This research points to dimensions of spiritual awareness as part of our inherent neurological being; it is not just the subjective result of our socially conditioned psychological being. Such research can open the way for scientists and others to take more seriously our spiritual nature. The great Jesuit scientist and theologian Pierre Teilhard de Chardin's summary of our nature is given greater credibility: "We are spiritual beings on a physical journey, not physical beings on a spiritual journey." Such a view has led some people today to explore what could be called neurotheology.[4]

THE POWER OF HABIT

While we're giving attention to our neurological structure, it's also worth noting the obvious but sometimes neglected power of habit in our lives. As we repeat behaviors, over time they are incorporated into the neurological patterns of our brain. Spiritual practices can become habits that burrow into our mental structure, shaping the ways we approach our days and respond to what we encounter. We all have developed habits that shape much of our lives. The spiritual question is: How do our habits shape our minds in a way that they are more open or closed to awareness of the living Presence?

For example, praying five times a day as a Muslim is a habit that inevitably impacts the mental structure of the prayer (the person praying), even though the person's rational interpretations of reality that may emerge from their prayer may differ from others with the same habit. Muslims, like fully observant Jews, have this common ground of conditioning that is meant to keep them attentive together to the larger Presence through the day, whatever their interpretations of their interior spiritual experience may be.

Christians, usually without the clear, shared daily prescription for prayer times that Muslims have, need to be more intentional in cultivating significant daily habits that sensitize us to the Spirit's living presence through the endless happenings of the day. This is especially important when we are in unsupportive cultural surroundings that easily bury such awareness. The particular habits we develop may become deadening at some point and need discerning revision as our spiritual journeys continue. Since we are creatures of habit, whatever habits we develop will affect the quality of our presence.

Neuroscientists who have examined the effects of meditation on the brain have had to change their views of neuroplasticity: the ability of the brain to restructure itself from experience. It's now clear that the brain can grow and redesign itself through training and other kinds of conditioning, even later in life. Thus, habits of meditation can truly be brain-changing.

THE IMPORTANCE OF CONTEMPLATIVE AWARENESS IN UNDERSTANDING THE MIND

One contribution of contemplative awareness to the scientific exploration of the mind is found in the frequent contemplative emphasis on a quality of self-less consciousness as a vital way of knowing reality. Francisco Varela, Evan Thompson, and Eleanor Rosch, three writers from different backgrounds, take this seriously in their groundbreaking exploration of this consciousness in relation to the mind, *The Embodied Mind*.[5] It is based on the view that only by having a sense of common ground between the "thinking" mind of the scientist and the "awareness" mind of the meditator can our understanding of cognition be more complete. The authors bring cognitive science, psychology, and philosophy into dialogue with Buddhist meditation practice and understanding.

Their fundamental insight is that we can see our mental activities as "reflections of a structure without losing sight of the directness of our own experience." Otherwise, we simply add layers of continued abstraction when we are restricted to the reflections, and lose the transformative awareness of mind that can show itself in deep meditation. That awareness contributes "an ever growing openness and lack of fixation." An openhearted sense of compassionate interest in others can replace the constant anxiety and irritation of egoistic concern.[6]

We can apply this basic insight to the relation of theological reflection and contemplative awareness as well. Theology, even more than science, needs to find common ground with contemplative awareness, given its ultimate grounding in firsthand spiritual experience, past and present. The theological mind has many needed gifts for us, and these gifts are at their best when the mind has remained close to the spiritual heart. When it hasn't, like the scientific mind it may find itself simply adding layers of continued abstraction, and perhaps falling into the danger of treating its concepts as though they could finally comprehend and exhaust deep Reality, about which they can but stutter. Part of theology's function is to protect the mystery of the divine, to not let it be reduced to less than it is. That more likely will be fulfilled when theologizing remains close to mature firsthand spiritual awareness: that of the theologian and of others recorded in the tradition and in our time.

I have spoken hopefully about some modern scientific tip-toeing toward appreciation of spiritual experience and first-hand contemplative awareness. This beachhead needs to be expanded among the great majority of scientists who, according to researchers such as B. Alan Wallace and Mario Beauregard, adhere to an essentially nonscientific metaphysics that in effect ignores any evidence that does not reduce reality to random physical and chemical phenomena. Closed to the possibility of these phenomena being vehicles of a larger purpose and consciousness, such scientists are in danger of fostering a comprehensive worldview of human beings as random biological creatures. Such a narrow view can negatively affect the way we see ourselves, treat others, and respond to the world's problems.

Science is a tremendously important, powerfully influential and exciting arena of human learning. For that very reason, those scientists who embrace scientific materialism need to be challenged and helped to see its unscientific character. They also need to examine its potentially skewing effect on their scientific work and teaching and, more broadly, its negative implications for human well-being.

The Impact of the Internet on Contemplative Awareness

One dramatic new way that science is massively affecting humanity is through the capacity it has given us to instantly find information on virtually any subject and to communicate with one another through the World Wide Web. This capacity has been received as a tremendous gift to us on many levels, as indeed it is. At the same time, we need to seriously ask the question about how it may be reshaping our brains. The Internet is such a relatively new and rapidly evolving phenomenon that there is much room for new research to be done. One of the things we are learning is that the instantaneous availability of infinite information blips seems to be reducing our capacity for sustained and reflective attention to any given subject.

Nicholas Carr speaks of this impact in a way that has significant implications for contemplative awareness. He sees an implied view of reality in what he calls "Google's world" that implicitly reduces wisdom to information/knowledge accumulation.

> In Google's world, the world we enter when we go online, there is little place for the fuzziness of contemplation. Ambiguity is nothing but a bug to be fixed. The human brain is just an outdated computer that needs a faster processor and a bigger hard drive....In the quiet spaces opened up by sustained, undistracted reading of a book, or by any other action of contemplation for that matter, we...draw out our own associations...and foster our own ideas. If we lose those quiet spaces, or fill them with "content," we will sacrifice something important not only in ourselves but in our culture.[7]

Wisdom in the fullest sense comes from deep, sustained listening with a dedication to the truth in both the thinking mind and in our spiritual hearts. As we find ourselves spending much time at multiple sites online, we need to assure ourselves regular, sure times when we allow for the sustained ambiguity of contemplative practice and reflection. Beyond short periods of set-aside practice each day and a general desire to be present to God through whatever we are doing during the day, we may need extended periods of intentional "fasting" from the Internet, as when we are on retreat or when we take quiet days during the year. This is doubly true if we're finding ourselves moving toward addiction to the Internet, turning to it in every spare moment for succor.

As we await more research on its impact on us, we know enough already to make sure that we're protecting space for the kind of open, direct presence that seeks the wisdom and peace that passes knowledge. In doing so, we can help assure room for connectedness with our deepest humanity and life in God.

Invitation to the Expanded Banquet Table

Everyone is called to the banquet of full life, awareness, love, and community, but who knows if we can trust the food and company, even if we're willing to let our familiar identities go by putting on a wedding garment? Today the banquet table is much larger than in earlier times. We have others close at hand at the table now who have brought the wine of their own spiritual vineyard. I expect Jesus, living as the universal Christ, the divine expression of loving Wisdom, would want us to find his Sophia-Spirit-presence in the newly visible wines on the table. After all, the divine Fount is One;[8] real spiritual wine flows from the same Source, matured in different vineyards and vintages. For example, if we want the contemplative wine in a passionately bubbly form, we can turn to Rumi, St. Francis, the Baal Shem Tov, and other passionate lovers at the table. If we want a calm, clear, multi-dimensional kind, we can turn to the Tibetan Buddhist sitting there, among others.

Tibetan Buddhism still is a relatively new frontier for most Christians.[9] By contrast, Zen Buddhism has had long-term exposure through Christian bridges, from the writings of Thomas Merton to those of a cadre of Jesuit missionaries who are or once were in Japan, among other Christians. Southeast Asian Theravada Buddhism has had a Christian bridge through the writings and many Carmelite-vipassana retreats of Mary Jo Meadow and a group of Carmelite priests. The international conferences and annual volume of *Buddhist-Christian Studies* have been a vital ongoing meeting ground of both practitioners and scholars probing the relationships of all schools of Buddhism and Christianity. In recent years, there have been a number of exchanges between Cistercian and Benedictine monastic communities, and Tibetan and other Buddhist monks.

One of the great gifts of a contemplative orientation is its capacity to attend our shared immediate open heart awareness, which precedes our different interpretations. That leaves us looking for connections with those traditions that pay attention to that preinterpretive level of awareness. The various contemplatively oriented strands of Buddhism share that attentiveness in many valuable ways. Even though I have found great value in the non-Tibetan forms of Buddhism to which I've been exposed over the years, I have found that the Tibetan tradition as a whole carries the widest range of practices and of careful cultivation of an understanding of contemplative awareness at the deepest levels, using all of our mental and physical human capacities in the process.

One accessible example of the adaptation of Buddhist-inspired contemplative awareness to Western culture is found in a book by the Tibetan lama Tarthang Tulku, Rinpoche, *Time, Space, and Knowledge: A New Vision of Reality*. Through experiential exercises and commentaries meant to be understandable to the scientific and philosophical Western mind, it offers a view of "Great Time, Great Space, and Great Knowledge." Through the firsthand experience of the exercises we are shown how incredibly constricted our way of approaching time, space, and knowledge normally has been. Our views of time, space, and knowledge control so much of the way we live and conceive of reality, including spiritual Reality.

Conclusion:
The Deepening Spiritual Journey

Many years ago I led a funeral service for Derek, the fourteen-week-old baby of close friends of mine. The cause of death was sudden infant death syndrome, which is something of a mystery to doctors. Derek seemed unusual in the arms of all who held him in the time he was alive—he had a quality of aged, mature serenity. As one of his parents said and others confirmed, he was like an old soul just passing through this life one more time for a brief while, and he felt like a blessing to each person.

We all pass through this mysterious life knowing that whether it is only for a few months or for one hundred years, sooner or later it will end in death to this life. Every day becomes precious. We have no hold on the future. We may have a plan for it, but it cannot be a controlling plan. Even if we don't die soon, others around us will die. Even as we continue to live, we nonetheless find ourselves dying to various stages of our life and understanding and rising to new ones. As St. Paul said, "Even though our outer nature is wasting away, our inner nature is being renewed day by day" (2 Cor 4:16).

We can't see over the hill ahead of us in our spiritual journey, although beyond the hill we can see the horizon, which is so open and alive. Others have walked the road before us, some walk with us now, and others will follow. The road is not straight. It spirals and meanders in unpredictable ways, and yet always the horizon is there, whichever way we are turned at the moment.

Contemplative awareness reminds us to see and trust the sacred Horizon that encompasses and pervades all we see, all we are. Death falls into this Horizon, as life falls out of it. This Horizon has no boundaries and includes all light and darkness. It mysteriously pulses with radiant Love that leads us to give it personal names. Then it is not only an *it* but also a *Thou*, whose image we mysteriously reflect, whose Being is in the core of our being. Contemplative awareness helps us to live into that Horizon in trust, receptive to the purging, loving Wisdom that frees us for our true being. As we're willing to live from that core of our being, we walk with Spirit-soaked footprints in the world, letting loving Light shine through us in myriad needed forms.

Notes

Chapter 1

1. William C. Chittick, *The Sufi Path of Love: The Spiritual Teachings of Rumi* (Albany: State University of New York Press, 1983), 221.

2. See Fordham theologian Craig Baron's reflections on this in "Christian Theology and the Re-enchantment of the World," *Cross Currents* (Winter 2007).

3. John Moyne and Coleman Barks, *Open Secret: Versions of Rumi* (Putney, VT: Threshold Books, 1984), #158.

4. Perhaps this connects with what the psalmist had in mind when he said: "The Lord knows our thoughts, that they are but an empty breath" (Ps 94:11).

5. For a brief history of Christian contemplative tradition, see chapter 4 in Thomas Keating, *Intimacy with God* (New York: Crossroad Publishing Company, 1997). He draws out a key biblical point: "To emphasize the experiential knowledge of God, the Greek Bible used the word *gnosis* to translate the Hebrew word *da'ath*, which implies a kind of intimate knowledge involving the whole person, not just the intellect (e.g., Ps. 130:1–6)." The early Greek fathers spoke of this knowledge being enabled by love. St. Paul affirms this in Philippians 1:9–10: "And this is my prayer, that your love may overflow more and more with knowledge and full insight to help you determine what is best...." We see his conviction of the fullness of knowledge that will be given us at

the end of life in 1 Corinthians 13:12: "Now I know only in part; then I will know fully, even as I have been fully known." For a way of looking at the different ways we "know" a spiritual experience, see chapter 2 in my *Spiritual Director, Spiritual Companion: Guide to Tending the Soul* (New York/Mahwah, NJ: Paulist Press, 2001).

6. One of the most enduring practices over the centuries in the tradition of the desert mothers and fathers was some form of the Jesus Prayer. The longest version is "Lord Jesus Christ, Son of God, have mercy on me, a sinner"; a shorter version would be "Lord Jesus Christ, have mercy on me" or even simply "Jesus, mercy." This might be done in rhythm with one's breathing. See my more detailed description and bibliographic references in *Living Simply through the Day: Spiritual Survival in a Complex Age* (New York/Mahwah, NJ: Paulist Press, 1988), 90–92.

7. E. Kadloubovsky and E. H. Palmer, trans., *The Art of Prayer: An Orthodox Anthology*, ed. Timothy Ware (London: Faber & Faber, 1966), 17.

8. See Marcus J. Borg's discussion of the biblical heart in chapter 5 in *The God We Never Knew: Beyond Dogmatic Religion to a More Authentic Contemporary Faith* (San Francisco: HarperSanFrancisco, 1997).

9. *Pseudo-Macarius: The Fifty Spiritual Homilies and the "Great Letter,"* Classics of Western Spirituality, trans. and ed. George A. Maloney, S.J. (New York/Mahwah, NJ: Paulist Press, 1992), 115–16.

10. "A Theological Perspective of Movement," *St. Vladimir's Theological Quarterly* 32, no. 1, 66. Chryssavgis goes on to say: "The intellect…becomes all eyes, riveting its waking, watching eyes on guarding its "treasure": God's presence dwelling in the heart….God's kingdom is within our heart (Lk 17:21)….In gathering the intellect to the heart in prayer, one does no more than respond to God with the love first given by Him. Yet one returns

it from one's emptiness, as priest, with thanks and glory, while He gives from His fullness."

11. Cynthia Bourgeault helpfully notes that "putting the mind in the heart" in Eastern Orthodox spirituality is traditionally accomplished by a "concentration of affectivity—or in other words by fanning the flames of the heart's native capacity for empathy, then concentrating this aroused emotion on the love of God." She notes that Centering Prayer (and I would add many other forms of contemplative prayer), building on an insight of Simeon the New Theologian (949–1022), suggests that "putting the mind in the heart can be accomplished just as effectively through kenosis, or the simple release of whatever you are clinging to,...releasing the passions and relaxing the will." See her *Centering Prayer and Inner Awakening* (Cambridge, MA: Cowley Publications, 2004), 41. She also elaborates on the heart in her insightful *The Wisdom Way of Knowing: Reclaiming an Ancient Tradition to Awaken the Heart* (San Francisco: Jossey-Bass, 2003).

12. It's also important to realize that calling them "mind" and "heart" is a simplifying heuristic device for speaking of two of the complex, different ways our consciousness touches deep Reality. The functions of mind and heart belong to one intimately connected multidimensional human capacity for awareness.

13. The Benedictine Mark O'Keefe says that the existence of an inner self, not fully available to our reflective consciousness, is a presupposition of traditional mystical literature. Thomas Merton describes the "true self" as "a shy, wild animal that can be glimpsed only in stillness and calm." That self is realized and authenticated in selfless loving. Our external "false self" carries our daily activities, everyday choices, virtues, and character, as if it encompasses the fullness of human existence, but it remains cut off from deep Reality to the extent that it carries on without cognizance of and conformity with the true self grounded in God. "Merton's 'True Self' and the Fundamental Option," in *The Merton Annual: Studies in Culture, Spirituality, and Social Concerns*, vol. 10,

ed. Victor A. Kramer (Collegeville, MN: Liturgical Press, 1998). See also Mark A. McIntosh, *Discernment and Truth: The Spirituality and Theology of Knowledge* (New York: Crossroad Publishing Company, 2004).

14. Bourgeault, *Centering Prayer*, 117.

Chapter 2

1. New York/Mahwah, NJ: Paulist Press, 1997.

2. New York/Mahwah, NJ: Paulist Press, 2001.

3. John S. Dunne, *The Way of All the Earth: Experiments in Truth and Religion* (Notre Dame, IN: University of Notre Dame Press, 1978), 9.

4. Raimon Panikkar, *The Experience of God: Icons of the Mystery* (Minneapolis: Fortress Press, 2006), 196ff.

5. For a thoughtful elaboration of the value of a panentheistic view as one that best accounts for spiritual experiences and best cuts through modern difficulties with a view of God as a supernatural being separate from the universe, see Marcus J. Borg, *The God We Never Knew: Beyond Dogmatic Religion to a More Authentic Contemporary Faith* (San Francisco: HarperSanFrancisco, 1997).

6. See "Partakers of the Divine Nature," in Timothy Ware, *The Orthodox Church* (New York: Penguin Books, 1964), 236–42.

7. For contemporary practical applications of Ignatius's process of discernment, see Thomas Green, S.J., *Weeds Among the Wheat* (Notre Dame, IN: Ave Marie Press, 1984); Maureen Conroy, R.S.M., *The Discerning Heart: Discovering a Personal God* (Chicago: Loyola Press, 1993). For a profound and fresh historical view of discernment that is sensitive to the contemplative/mystical ground, see Mark A. McIntosh, *Discernment and Truth: The Spirituality and Theology of Knowledge* (New York: Crossroad Publishing Company, 2004). For a fine succinct, contemplatively

grounded view of discernment, see Rose Mary Dougherty, *Discernment: A Path to Spiritual Awakening* (New York/Mahwah, NJ: Paulist Press, 2009).

8. For a fuller background on icons, see their description in chapter 4 of my *Living in the Presence: Spiritual Exercises to Open Our Lives to the Awareness of God* (San Francisco: Harper-SanFrancisco, 1995), which also includes a select bibliography in the footnotes. (To those books I would add these: Linette Martin, *Sacred Doorways: A Beginner's Guide to Icons* [Brewster, MA: Paraclete Press, 2002]; Jim Forest, *Praying with Icons* [Maryknoll, NY: Orbis Books, 1997]; and Paul Evdokimov, *The Art of the Icon: A Theology of Beauty* [Redondo Beach, CA: Oakwood Publications, 1990].)

9. For a larger context of the body and prayer, see chapter 2 and exercises 1 and 2 in my *Living in the Presence*.

Chapter 3

1. Raimon Panikkar insightfully says that an experience of God "is not my experience of God but God's experience in me and through me of which I am conscious....I understand my participation in that experience as a communion...between God, who is the subject, and that experience of God that is mine to the degree that I become conscious of it." *The Experience of God: Icons of the Mystery* (Minneapolis: Fortress Press, 2006), 57–58.

Chapter 4

1. A symptom of this growth is the explosive increase in the membership of Spiritual Directors International, which publishes lists of available spiritual directors, holds a huge annual meeting, has spawned many regional groups, and publishes *Presence* and other materials. Its Web site is http://www.sdiworld.

org. There also has been a burgeoning number of programs that assist in the development of spiritual directors who are called to this ministry. Shalem Institute's Spiritual Guidance Program, which began in 1978, was one of the first.

2. I discuss rules of life briefly in my *Spiritual Director, Spiritual Companion: Guide to Tending the Soul* (New York/ Mahwah, NJ: Paulist Press, 2001), 85. See also *The Rule of the Society of Saint John the Evangelist* (Cambridge, MA: Cowley Publications, 1997) for an example of what a contemporary American religious community has done to develop a viable modern rule of life. Many of its features provide fresh insight for any intentional rule of life.

3. See, for example, Ian Bradley, *Colonies of Heaven: Celtic Models for Today's Church* (London: Darton, Longman & Todd, 2000), and Jerry C. Doherty, *A Celtic Model of Ministry: The Reawakening of Community Spirituality* (Collegeville, MN: Liturgical Press, 2003). David Keller, an Episcopal priest, has helped to found a new contemplative community model that exists in a number of places in the United States now. They are ecumenical, informal, Benedictine and Celtic-influenced communities in the United States whose members, among other things, need to be active in a parish church, can take temporary vows, and can be married or single.

4. *Mathnawi* II:1770, quoted in William C. Chittick, *The Sufi Path of Love: The Spiritual Teachings of Rumi* (Albany: State University of New York Press, 1983), 213.

5. Diana Butler Bass, *The Practicing Congregation: Imagining a New Old Church* (Herndon, VA: The Alban Institute, 2004), 59–63. This book is a very insightful study of the spectrum of contemporary congregational life and values within a larger cultural and historical framework, with special emphasis on and hope for evolving mainline Protestant congregations.

6. David Keller's passionate commitment to such a view of the congregation has been influential in my thinking.

7. Robert Duggan is a Roman Catholic priest. In a class lecture at Shalem Institute, he said, "Since the life of the local congregation is the primary vehicle for spiritual formation, clergy leaders who wish to be intentional about the work of spiritual formation must seek to promote a contemplative grounding that permeates every aspect of the community's life."

8. Some of this is found in more detailed form in Duggan's article "Parish as a Center for Forming a Spiritual People," *New Theology Review* 11 (1998): 14–27.

9. Isaac of Nineveh, *Mystic Treatises*, ed. and trans. A. J. Wensinck (Amsterdam: Koninklijke Akademie van Wetenschappen, 2007).

10. Excerpts from a lecture, "The Eucharist and Silence," delivered on April 20, 2005, at the School of Prayer in the Archdiocese of Melbourne.

11. See chapter 3 in my *Living in the Presence: Spiritual Exercises to Open Our Lives to the Awareness of God* (San Francisco: HarperSanFrancisco, 1995) for more on sound and silence. For a simple form of contemplative Eucharist that I developed some years ago, using few words and much silence, see "Tilden Edwards' Thoughts" under Publications at www.shalem.org.

Chapter 5

1. Gandhi listed the seven deadly social sins as politics without principle, wealth without work, commerce without morality, pleasure without conscience, education without character, science without humanity, and worship without sacrifice.

2. I further develop this understanding in the context of peacemaking in "Spiritual Perspectives on Peacemaking," a chapter in E. Glenn Hinson, ed., *Spirituality in Ecumenical Perspective* (Louisville: Westminster/John Knox Press, 1993).

3. I'm indebted to Susan Murphy, a regional Shalem Institute staff member, for several of the basic themes of these practices, although I have adapted them as practices in my own way.

4. Gerald G. May, *Will and Spirit: A Contemplative Psychology* (San Francisco: Harper & Row, 1982), 149–60. I highly recommend reading the whole chapter "Love: The Answer to Fear."

5. From Paul Evdokimov, *The Art of the Icon: A Theology of Beauty* (Redondo Beach, CA: Oakwood Publications, 1990).

6. Cited in the periodical *The Sun*, November 1993, without further reference.

7. May, *Will and Spirit*, 155–56.

8. For Asian resources specifically related or adapted to a Christian context, see Philip St. Romain, *Kundalini Energy and Christian Spirituality: A Pathway to Growth and Healing*, with a foreword by Thomas Keating (New York: Crossroad Publishing Company, 1991); Thomas Ryan, *Prayer of the Heart and Body: Meditation and Yoga as Christian Spiritual Practice* (New York/Mahwah, NJ: Paulist Press, 1995); Nancy Roth, *The Breath of God: An Approach to Prayer* (Cambridge, MA: Cowley Publications, 1990); and Linda Sabbath, *The Radiant Heart* (Denville, NJ: Dimension Books, 1977). A book that includes some Christian authors speaking of sexuality in a larger context of eros and spirituality is Georg Feuerstein, ed., *Enlightened Sexuality: Essays on Body-Positive Spirituality* (Freedom, CA: The Crossing Press, 1989).

9. "The Challenge of Ecojustice," *The Witness*, September 1990.

10. For a brief inspiring and biblically grounded example of such writings, I particularly recommend James Hall, "Reclaiming the Body of the Earth," in Thomas Ryan, ed., *Reclaiming the Body in Christian Spirituality* (New York/Mahwah, NJ: Paulist Press, 2004). His notes at the end include many other books. Among many other fine writings, I would mention Thomas Berry, *The*

Dream of the Earth (San Francisco: Sierra Club Books, 1988); Jay B. McDaniel, *With Roots and Wings: Christianity in an Age of Ecology and Dialogue* (Maryknoll, NY: Orbis Books, 1995); Michael Dowd, *Earthspirit: A Handbook for Nurturing an Ecological Christianity* (Twenty-Third Publications, 1991); Elizabeth Roberts and Elias Amidon, *Earth Prayers: From around the World, 365 Prayers, Poems, and Invocations for Honoring the Earth* (San Francisco: HarperSanFrancisco, 1991); and Judy Cannato, *Radical Amazement: Contemplative Lessons from Black Holes, Supernovas, and Other Wonders of the Universe* (Notre Dame, IN: Sorin Books, 2006).

11. Brian Swimme and Thomas Berry, *The Universe Story: From the Primordial Flaring Forth to the Ecozoic Era—A Celebration of the Unfolding of the Cosmos* (San Francisco: HarperSanFrancisco, 1992), 245, 255.

12. For example, see also Brian Swimme, *The Hidden Heart of the Cosmos: Humanity and the New Story* (Maryknoll, NY: Orbis Books, 1999), and Diarmuid O'Murchu, *Evolutionary Faith: Rediscovering God in Our Great Story* (Maryknoll, NY: Orbis Books, 2002).

13. O'Murchu, *Evolutionary Faith*, 266.

14. *The Wisdom of Wilderness: Experiencing the Healing Power of Nature* (San Francisco: HarperSanFrancisco, 2006).

15. Written scientific and theological descriptions became possible with the invention of the alphabet, but as someone has noted, the price of learning the alphabet was the loss of direct, participative knowledge.

16. Swimme and Berry, *The Universe Story*, 264.

17. In terms of the *hara*, the only book I know that's fully dedicated to it is Karlfried Graf Dürckheim, *Hara: The Vital Center of Man* (Rochester, VT: Inner Traditions, 2004). See also James Deacon's Reiki Web site, http://www.aetw.org.

18. Rose Mary Dougherty of the Shalem Institute staff was the first person to expose me to this form of intercession. What you read here is my own interpretation.

Chapter 6

1. The full text of the document is available online at http://www.vatican.va/archive/hist_councils/ii_vatican_council/documents/vat-ii_const_19641121_lumen-gentium_en.html.

Chapter 7

1. An example of this larger movement is seen in Korea. In its extension programs, the Shalem Institute has had a number of Korean pastors from four different Christian traditions. One of them spoke for all of them when he said, in effect, that contemplative understanding and practice represent the missing depth dimension in their own formation and that of their congregations. Shalem has responded to the request of some of them to begin a contemplatively oriented extension program in Korea, primarily for clergy.

2. Eboo Patel, *Acts of Faith: The Story of an American Muslim, the Struggle for the Soul of a Generation* (Boston: Beacon Press, 2007).

3. Ministry of Money, "Programs," http://www.ministryof money.org/Programs.htm.

4. Ian Bradley says that pilgrimage is the most important and distinctive theme of Celtic Christianity. In symbolic terms, it "was a favorite metaphor to express the Celtic emphasis on the dynamic character of Christian faith." Bradley provides many excellent insights into this early Christian tradition, including its understanding of pilgrimage as both an inner state of mind and an outward form of journeying. See his chapter "Pilgrimage" in

Colonies of Heaven: Celtic Models for Today's Church (London: Darton, Longman & Todd, 2000).

Chapter 8

1. George E. Vaillant, *Spiritual Evolution: A Scientific Defense of Faith* (New York: Broadway Books, 2008).

2. *The God Gene: How Faith Is Hardwired into Our Genes* (New York: Doubleday, 2004).

3. Reported in, "If It Feels Good to Be Good, It Might Be Only Natural," an article by Shankar Vedantam in the May 28, 2007, issue of the *Washington Post*, A1. The neuroscientist researchers from the National Institutes of Health are Jorge Moll and Jordan Grafman.

4. Books relating to neurotheology include Matthew Alper, *The "God" Part of the Brain: A Scientific Interpretation of Human Spirituality and God* (Naperville, IL: Sourcebooks, 2006); Rhawn Joseph, ed., *NeuroTheology: Brain, Science, Spirituality, Religious Experience* (San Jose, CA: University Press, 2003); Jensine Andresen, ed., *Religion in Mind: Cognitive Perspectives on Religious Belief, Ritual, and Experience* (Cambridge: Cambridge University Press, 2001); and Todd Tremlin, *Minds and Gods: The Cognitive Foundations of Religion* (New York: Oxford University Press, 2006).

5. Francisco J. Varela, Evan Thompson, and Eleanor Rosch, *The Embodied Mind: Cognitive Science and Human Experience* (Cambridge, MA: MIT Press, 1991).

6. Ibid., 234.

7. "Is Google Making Us Stupid?" *The Atlantic*, August 2008, 63.

8. I first saw the term *Fount* used for God the Creator/Father in an article by the theologian Robert Hughes, "After the Empire: Mission in the Power of the Spirit," *Sewanee Theological*

Review 50 (Pentecost 2007); his source may have been Robert W. Jenson, *Systematic Theology*, vol. 1, *The Triune God* (New York: Oxford University Press, 1997).

    9. When I wrote a chapter for Tarthang Tulku, ed., *Reflections of Mind: Western Psychology Meets Tibetan Buddhism*, Nyingma Psychology Series (Berkeley: Dharma Publishing, 1975), I knew of nothing written at that time about Tibetan Buddhism in relation to Christianity, except for Thomas Merton's experience with a Tibetan Buddhist hermit, found in *The Asian Journal of Thomas Merton* (New York: New Directions Publishing, 1973).

Spiritual Friend
Reclaiming the Gift of Spiritual Direction
Tilden Edwards
A practical guide to reviving the ancient Christian
tradition of the spiritual guide.
0-8091-2288-X   Paperback

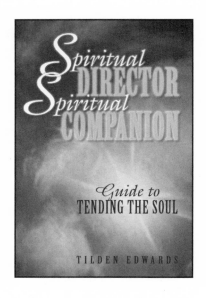

Spiritual Director, Spiritual Companion

Guide to Tending the Soul

Tilden Edwards

A guide to spiritual direction with emphasis on its practical, historical and theological grounding, by a leading expert in spiritual companionship.

0-8091-4011-X   Paperback

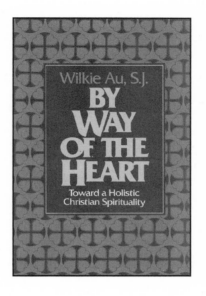

By Way of the Heart
Toward a Holistic Christian Spirituality
Wilkie Au
A contemporary guidebook for the
spiritual journey, steeped in the Christian tradition
and rich in psychological insight.
0-8091-3118-8   Paperback

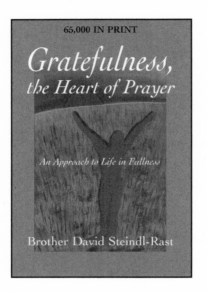

65,000 IN PRINT

Gratefulness,
the Heart of Prayer

An Approach to Life in Fullness

Brother David Steindl-Rast

Gratefulness, the Heart of Prayer

An Approach to Life in Fullness
Brother David Steindl-Rast, OSB
A monk reflects on the many aspects of the spiritual life
with the basic attitude of gratefulness.

"A true delight."
—Henri J. M. Nouwen

0-8091-2628-1   Paperback

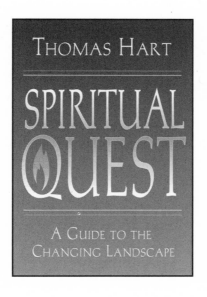

Spiritual Quest
A Guide to the Changing Landscape
Thomas N. Hart
A guide for those who want to grow in the spiritual life,
with insights into the questions spawned
by today's spiritual resurgence.
0-8091-3906-5   Paperback

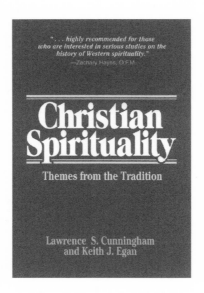

"... *highly recommended for those who are interested in serious studies on the history of Western spirituality.*"
—Zachary Hayes, O.F.M.

Christian Spirituality

Themes from the Tradition

Lawrence S. Cunningham
and Keith J. Egan

Christian Spirituality
Themes from the Tradition
Lawrence S. Cunningham and Keith J. Egan
A concise and accessible thematic overview of the
various ways Christians have approached God
in prayer and practice.
0-8091-3660-0   Paperback

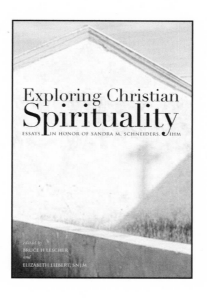

Exploring Christian Spirituality

Essays in Honor of Sandra M. Schneiders, IHM
Edited by Bruce H. Lescher and Elizabeth Liebert, SNJM
In this book, leading scholars address issues of
methodology and interdisciplinarity that are emerging at
the creative "edges" of the academic discipline of
Christian spirituality.
0-8091-4216-3   Paperback

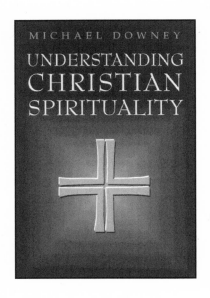

Understanding Christian Spirituality

Michael Downey

A readable overview of the contemporary spiritual scene
that defines, outlines and advocates several models or
methods for studying Christian spirituality with a
respect for Scripture, tradition, and one's own
personal and cultural experiences.

0-8091-3680-5   Paperback

Spiritual Masters for All Seasons
Michael Ford
Invites four spiritual masters onto the same stage for the
first time and shows how they speak—Thomas Merton,
Henri Nouwen, Anthony de Mello, and John
O'Donahue—while assessing their place in the
world of contemporary spirituality.

978-1-58768-055-7   Paperback

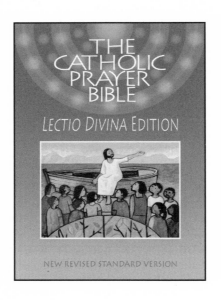

The Catholic Prayer Bible (NRSV):
Lectio Divina Edition

An ideal Bible for anyone who desires to reflect on the
individual stories and chapters of just one, or even all,
of the biblical books, while being led to prayer
though meditation on that biblical passage.

978-0-8091-0587-8   Hardcover
978-0-8091-4663-5   Paperback

green press
INITIATIVE

Paulist Press is committed to preserving ancient forests and natural resources. We elected to print this title on 30% post consumer recycled paper, processed chlorine free. As a result, for this printing, we have saved:

4 Trees (40' tall and 6-8" diameter)
1 Million BTUs of Total Energy
363 Pounds of Greenhouse Gases
1,750 Gallons of Wastewater
106 Pounds of Solid Waste

Paulist Press made this paper choice because our printer, Thomson-Shore, Inc., is a member of Green Press Initiative, a nonprofit program dedicated to supporting authors, publishers, and suppliers in their efforts to reduce their use of fiber obtained from endangered forests.

For more information, visit www.greenpressinitiative.org

Environmental impact estimates were made using the Environmental Defense Paper Calculator. For more information visit: www.papercalculator.org.